CHILDREN'S CREATIVE CRAFT PROJECTS

A FUN WAY FOR CHILDREN AND ADULTS TO BE CREATIVE TOGETHER

MARGARET ETHERINGTON

Tuva Publishing

www.tuvapublishing.com

Address

Merkez Mah. Cavusbasi Cad. No:71

Cekmekoy - Istanbul 34782 / Turkey

Tel: +9 0216 642 62 62

Children's Creative Craft Projects

First Print

2019 / March

All Global Copyrights Belong To

Tuva Tekstil ve Yayıncılık Ltd.

Content

Craft

Editor in Chief

Ayhan DEMİRPEHLİVAN

Project Editor

Kader DEMİRPEHLİVAN

Designer

Margaret ETHERINGTON

Technical Editors

Leyla ARAS

Büşra ESER

Graphic Designers

Ömer ALP

Abdullah BAYRAKÇI

Zilal ÖNEL

Photograph

Tuva Publishing

Printed in Turkey

ISBN

978-605-9192-58-3

 TuvaYayincilik  TuvaPublishing

TuvaYayincilik  TuvaPublishing

INTRODUCTION

The projects in this book will appeal to school-age children from the very young to mid-teens and beyond. In addition to making items on their own, some may also choose to do crafting with carers, parents or other adults in order to share skills. Children gain understanding and confidence from 'in the moment' support, and are subsequently able to tackle more intricate tasks by themselves.

The book is designed to include many craft ideas that involve recycling fabric and other remnants, as well as re-using packaging. It also recognises that widely available products such as unvarnished boxes and blank greetings cards offer a shortcut to making crafts accessible to the beginner. Not everyone is brilliant with scissors, so there are options to replace a template with a craft punch, which can be purchased in shops or online.

To increase the young maker's confidence further, numerous templates are provided to ensure they can be proud of their early projects. Once they have had the hands-on experience of using techniques successfully, crafters can adapt what they have learned to produce their own original ideas in the future.

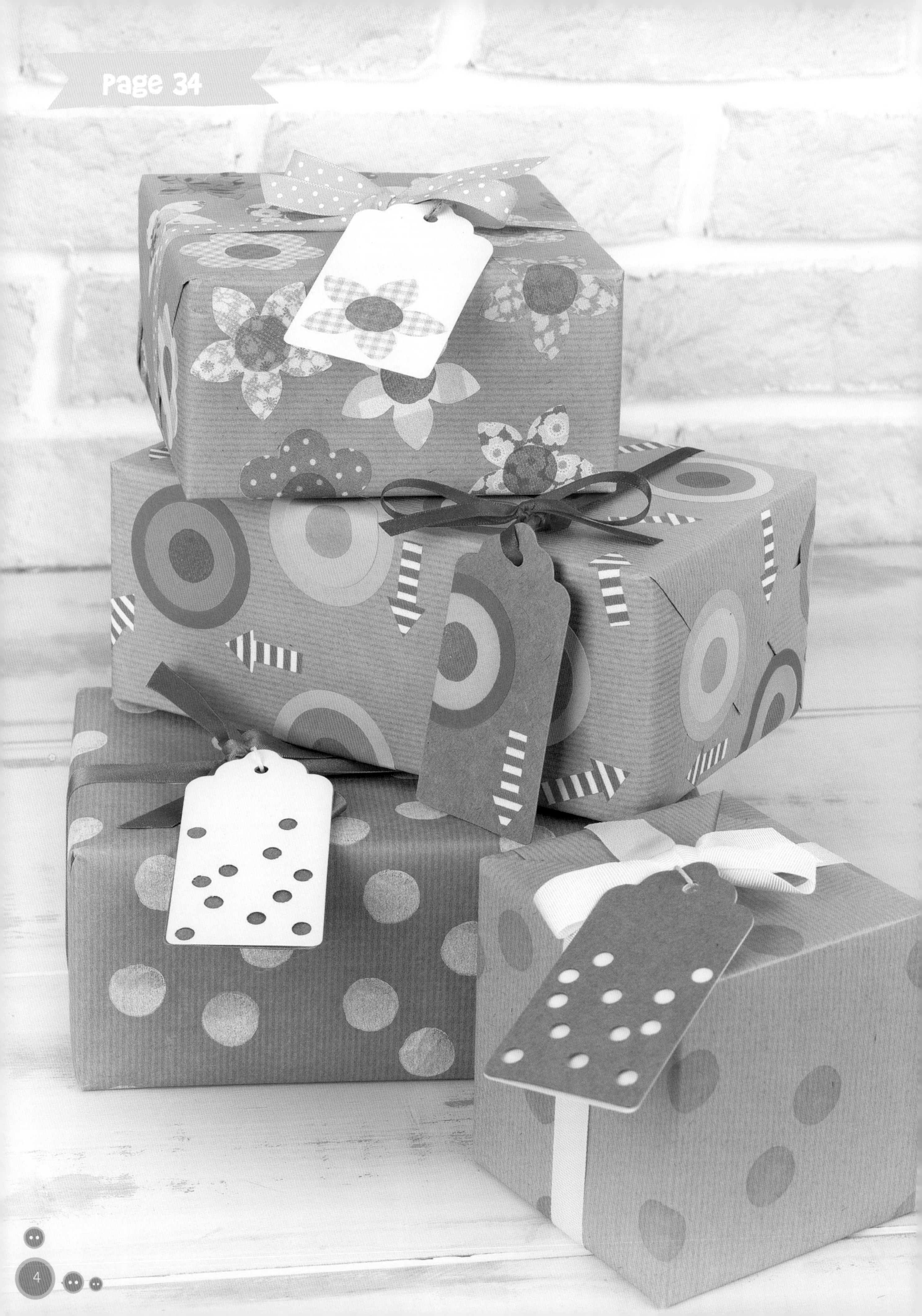

Page 34

CONTENTS

TEMPLATES

STAMPED

AND Stencilled
Tissue Boxes

Customise unvarnished tissue boxes by painting through a stencil,
or stamping a pencil eraser onto a strip of fabric.

TIP A very quick stencil can be made using a craft punch for the
flower shape, to save cutting it out.

For the square green rabbit box, you will need:

Materials

- A wooden unfinished tissue box cover with a sliding base
- White emulsion paint
- Optional: fine sandpaper
- Light green emulsion paint
- 100% plain cotton fabric, in cream
- Rabbit stencil
- Circular template with centre cut away
- Removable glue dots
- Grey emulsion paint
- Decoupage glue, matt
- A4 size (8.5" x 11") thin card

Equipment

- Small decorators' paintbrush
- Scissors
- Either small-hole punch or a bradawl
- Small foam paint roller and tray
- Pair of compasses
- Pencil
- Ruler
- Pinking shears

1 Coat the exterior of the box with white emulsion, painting only the parts that will be seen in the finished item, not the base or inside. When dry, check for any rough areas that need sanding, especially inside the hole at the top.

Then paint on 2 coats of light green emulsion.

2 On the stencil, pierce the rabbit's eye to make a round hole. Ideally, use a small-hole punch for neatness.

3 Place a removable glue dot on the back of the rabbit and press it onto the fabric.

4 Using compasses, draw a 6cm (2.4″) diameter circle in the middle of the sheet of card. Cut out.

On the back of the card, stick a glue dot above and below the round hole.

Position the card on the fabric so that the rabbit appears centrally within the hole.

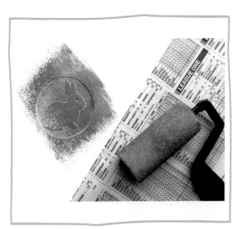

5 With the roller, apply grey paint to the visible fabric. A light area blending into a darker one will give you an interesting variety of tone.

6 When the paint is dry, remove the card stencils.

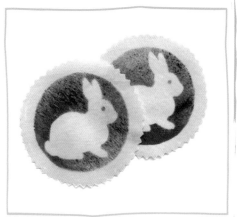

7 Place the circular template precisely on top of the rabbit motif

8 Draw in pencil around the outside of the template. Repeat the above process to produce 3 further stencilled rabbits.

9 With pinking shears, cut on the insides of the pencil lines.

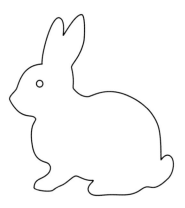

Original Size

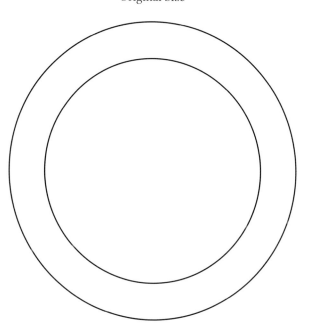

10 Brush decoupage glue over the central area of one of the box sides. Before it dries, place a fabric rabbit in the middle, checking your accuracy with a ruler. Brush more glue on top of the fabric, continuing to the edges of the box surface.

Repeat with the other 3 sides, and then brush the top with glue to varnish it.

When dry, your cover is ready to use by sliding open the base and inserting a box of tissues.

Materials

- ⚑ A wooden unfinished tissue box cover with a sliding base
- ⚑ White emulsion paint
- ⚑ Optional: fine sandpaper
- ⚑ Light green and very pale green emulsion paint
- ⚑ 100% plain cotton fabric, in pink
- ⚑ Decoupage glue, matt

Equipment

- ⚑ Small decorators' paintbrush
- ⚑ White plastic eraser
- ⚑ Craft or kitchen knife
- ⚑ Small chopping board
- ⚑ Mauve or lilac stamp pad
- ⚑ Ruler
- ⚑ Pencil
- ⚑ Fabric scissors

1 Coat the exterior of the box with white emulsion, painting only the parts that will be seen in the finished item, not the base or inside. When dry, check for any rough areas that need sanding, especially inside the hole at the top.

2 Draw a pencil line around the box, 3cm (1.2") up from the bottom. Apply 2 coats of the darker paint above the line, and 2 coats of the lighter paint below it.

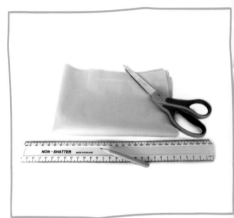

3 Select a piece of fabric long enough to go right around your tissue box. With the ruler and pencil, draw a straight line along the grain of the fabric. Then draw a parallel line 2cm (.8") away from the first one. Cut out this strip with fabric scissors.

4 Chop a rectangular piece off the eraser to make a stamp. Make it slightly wedge-shaped, like a thin pineapple chunk.

5 Press the stamp into the ink pad and print onto the fabric at right angles to the raw edges. Repeat along the fabric strip, inking the stamp afresh each time you print. Sometimes, turn the stamp upside down; also, make the gaps in between the prints irregular for added interest and variety. Allow the ink to dry.

6 You will be sticking the fabric to each side of the box as one long strip, and overlapping it when you get back to the beginning. The bottom of the strip will be 2cm (.8") above the box base, so keep checking this measurement with the ruler as you stick down the fabric.

Brush decoupage glue along the lower part of one box side, and apply the fabric strip. Repeat on the other 3 sides until you have a continuous trim all the way round.

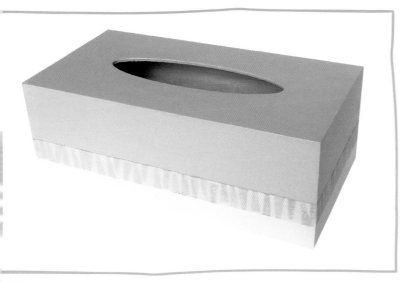

7 Apply glue to the whole box exterior, including on top of the fabric. When dry, your cover is ready to use by sliding open the base and inserting a box of tissues.

Materials

- A wooden unfinished tissue box cover with a sliding base
- White emulsion paint
- Optional: fine sandpaper
- Pale pink and darker pink emulsion paint
- Circular template with centre cut away (see page 9)
- Optional: flower stencil if not using craft punch
- Optional: piece of thin card
- 100% cotton polka dot fabric
- 100% cotton plain fabric, in cream
- Decoupage glue, matt
- Masking tape 25mm (1″) wide
- Small round adhesive label. If you don't have one of these, you could use a hole punch on the sticky part of a post-it note. Put two sticky sides together before punching.

Equipment

- Small decorators' paintbrush
- Optional: large flower craft punch, or cut out a stencil by hand
- Fabric scissors
- Small foam paint roller and tray
- Pencil
- Ruler
- Pinking shears

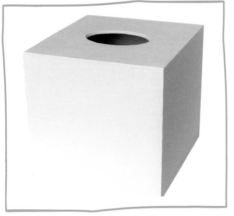

1 Paint the tissue box with white emulsion. When dry, smooth any rough areas with fine sandpaper. Add two coats of pale pink emulsion.

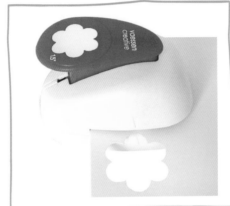

2 Punch a flower shape into thin card, or cut out the stencil by hand.

3 Trim the card around the cut-out.

4 Place the flower stencil on the polka dot fabric and stick down with masking tape.

5 Stick a small, round adhesive label in the middle of the flower.

6 Load up the paintbrush with generous amounts of the darker pink paint and transfer to the roller tray. Roll the sponge back and forwards in the tray until well covered with paint, and then repeat this action onto the stencil.

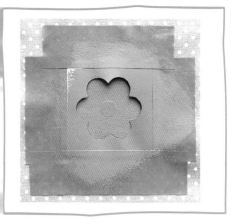

7 Ensure a good coverage of paint within the stencil area. Allow to dry.

8 Remove the masking tape and round label.

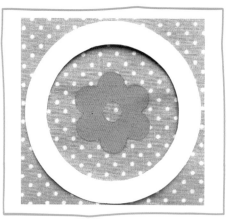

9 Position the circular template so that the flower appears centrally within it. Check your accuracy with a ruler. Holding the card ring in place firmly, draw around the inside of it with a pencil.

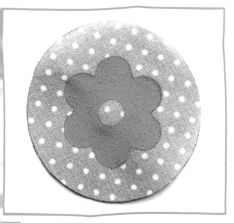

10 Cut out the pencil circle with fabric scissors.

Repeat 3 more times to produce a flower motif for each side of the tissue box.

11 On the plain fabric, draw around the outside of the ring template 4 times in pencil. Cut out with pinking shears on the inside of the pencil circles.

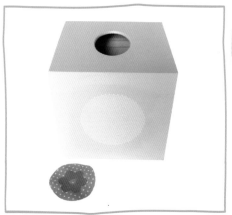

12 Brush some decoupage glue onto one face of the tissue box and position a plain fabric shape centrally. Brush more glue on top, and add the flower motif, also in a central position. Continue brushing the glue over the whole box side, including on top of the flower. Repeat on the other box faces. Apply glue to the box top as well, to varnish it.

13 Allow to dry, and finish by inserting a box of paper tissues.

Original Size

Stamping, stencilling and Printing

BLOCK
Printing

Potato prints have a new look, based on a simple triangle. Printing is also made easy by cutting craft foam with scissors and sticking onto a block.

TIP Instead of pricey fabric paint for the T-shirts, equal quantities of acrylic paint and fabric medium work just as well.

15

To print pink and
red hearts onto
a T-shirt,
you will need:

Materials

- 1 white 100% cotton T-shirt
- Small self-adhesive foam sheet
- 3 heart-shaped templates
- 2 clear acrylic blocks
- Pink fabric paint
- Red fabric paint
- A few wooden cocktail sticks
- Adhesive parcel tape
- Masking tape
- White cotton fabric remnant for practice
- Old newspapers to protect surfaces

Equipment

- Scissors
- Pencil
- 2 chopping boards covered in plastic bags
- 2 old washing up sponges
- Ruler

1 Trace around the 3 heart-shaped templates onto the foam sheet's backing paper. Cut out the foam shapes.

2 Peel off the paper backing and stick the foam shapes onto the acrylic blocks.

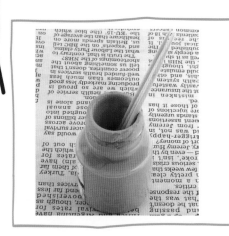 

3 Add a few drops of water to the pink fabric paint if using for the first time. Stir with 2 or 3 cocktail sticks.

4 Spread the paint onto a covered chopping board using the sides of the sticks.

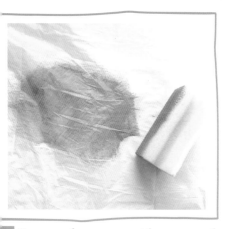

5 Dampen the sponge with water and squeeze until almost dry. Pick up the paint with the smooth side of the sponge, and dab it onto the larger heart block.

6 Press the block onto the fabric remnant, and allow the paint to dry.

7 Repeat the printing process with the smaller heart and some red fabric paint.

8 The red heart should be positioned centrally atop the pink one.
When you have finished practising, prepare a T-shirt for printing.

9 Insert the second covered board into the T-shirt, pulling it taut across the front area. Tape the sleeves, sides and bottom at the back of the board.

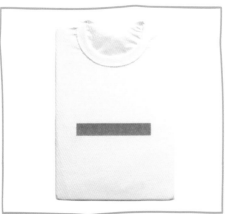

10 Stick a piece of masking tape centrally and horizontally on the T-shirt front, the width of 3 large heart blocks. The top edge of the tape should be lined up with the base of the block each time you print.

11 Print 3 pink hearts and allow to dry. Add 3 small red hearts to complete the design. Again, leave to dry.

Follow the paint manufacturer's instructions for setting the colours with an iron so that the T-shirt can be laundered.

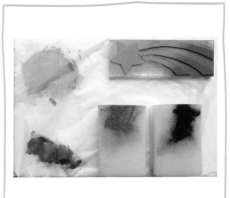

1 To print a shooting star onto a T-shirt, use the same process as for the hearts T-shirt.

From the star template, make the printing block as you did before.

2 There are 2 colours on the star block, blending into each other. Apply blue and purple paint to the board, and pick it up with a different sponge for each colour.

Dab blue paint onto most of the foam star and 'tail'. Then dab purple onto the end of the star's tail, and overlap purple paint onto some of the blue paint, as shown.

Try this out on a fabric remnant first, to make sure you achieve a good colour blend.

3 Repeat the T-shirt preparation and print the block onto the front as a single motif.

Press with an iron as previously.

To make a table placemat, you will need:

Materials

- White 100% cotton square napkin, pressed with an iron
- A washed potato
- 2 triangular templates
- Acrylic paints in yellow, red and turquoise
- Fabric or textile medium
- Old newspapers to protect surfaces

Equipment

- Vegetable knife and small chopping board
- Heat-erasable pen (the outline disappears when pressed with a hot iron)
- Paintbrush
- 3 plastic pots for mixing paint

1 Cut a potato in half and hold a triangular template onto the freshly cut surface. Ask someone to help you make 3 straight cuts with the knife along each side of the triangle to a depth of about 1cm (.5″).

Remove the template and trim off pieces of the potato around the triangle.

2 Mix the acrylic paint colours with equal quantities of fabric medium. The medium prevents the acrylic paint from drying too quickly.

Paint the colour onto the potato motif each time you print it onto the fabric.

3 Draw 3 lines onto the cotton napkin with the heat-erasable pen.

Start printing yellow triangles with the short edges on the pen line. When you have printed 3 of them, leave a space the width of a template, then print more yellow shapes.

4 Wash the potato under a running tap, and dab dry. Print turquoise shapes in the gaps you left. When finished, let the 2 paint colours dry thoroughly.

5 Wash and dry the potato again. Cut lines into the potato's surface with the knife angled to make 'V' shaped incisions. This will help you to lift out the waste potato.

Instead of cutting the pattern as straight lines, make them a bit crooked, as shown.

Brush red acrylic paint sparingly onto the potato surface. You will need less paint this time.

6 Print the red shapes onto 2 out of 3 yellow triangles. When dry, iron to remove the pen lines and to set the colour.

Pin Cushion
FRIDGE
Magnets

Pretty miniature cushions can be stuck on a fridge to hold pins, needles and badges.

TIP Keep them in your own room by attaching the cushions to a couple of enamel mugs containing small accessories.

Materials

- Felt fabric remnants
- 100% cotton fabric remnants, patterned
- 100% cotton fabric, plain
- Polyester filling or stuffing fibre
- 4 wooden rabbit buttons
- Sewing threads
- 8 x 20mm (.8″) sticky magnet dots

Equipment

- Sewing machine
- Pinking shears
- Fabric scissors
- Needle and pins
- Ruler
- Iron for pressing

Cutting

Felt shapes with a pinked edge, as follows:

1 x circle 5.4cm (2″) diameter
1 x rectangle 4.2 cm x 6 cm (1.6″ x 2.4″)
1 x square 3.8 cm x 3.8 cm (1.5″ x 1.5″)
1 x square 4.6 cm x 4.6 cm (1.8″ x 1.8″)

Fabric squares and rectangles in 4 different patterns:

2 squares 7.5cm x 7.5 cm (3″ x 3″)
2 squares 7.5cm x 7.5 cm (3″ x 3″)
2 squares 6.4 cm x 6.4 cm (2.5″ x 2.5″)
2 rectangles 6.8 cm x 10 cm (2.7″ x 4″)

Plain fabric squares and rectangles for the inner cushion pads:

4 squares 7.5cm x 7.5 cm (3″ x 3″)
2 squares 6.4 cm x 6.4 cm (2.5″ x 2.5″)
2 rectangles 6.8 cm x 10 cm (2.7″ x 4″)

1 To make a case for one of the inner cushion pads, place 2 same-sized cotton shapes together, and machine stitch 6mm (.25″) away from the edge on 3 sides. On the 4th side, fold the fabric outwards to a depth of 6 mm (.25"). Press the fold with an iron.

Repeat for the other 3 pad cases.

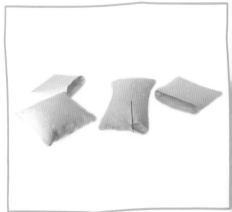

2 Snip off the corners furthest from the ironed fold (avoiding the stitching) and turn the cases inside out. Stuff with the filling fibre. Hand sew the gaps closed with tiny slip stitches.

3 Take one fabric square or rectangle in each pattern. Place a felt shape on each, positioning centrally. Machine stitch onto the patterned piece in contrasting thread.

Hand sew the buttons onto the double layer of fabric.

4 With the right sides of patterned fabric together, stitch and press in the same way as for the inner pads. This time the seam allowance is slightly less: 5mm (.2").

Insert pads into the correct cushion covers. Remove an adhesive magnet dot from its backing, and stick onto the back of the cushion. Take a second magnet dot, and carefully insert between the pad and the inside of the cushion cover. Stick precisely under the first dot, so there is a single layer of fabric between the 2 magnets. Press firmly together.

5 Close the openings in all 4 cushions with tiny slip stitches in a matching thread. Keep on the fridge, or other metal surface.

Seam – Free Patchwork

CUSHION

Patchwork is produced quickly by bonding fabric remnants to a ready-made cover.

TIP Inexpensive covers can be irregular shapes, so don't assume yours is a perfect square; position all of the patches first, before starting to iron them down.

To make the cushion with square patches and buttons, you will need:

Materials

- 100% percale cotton zipped cushion cover 35.5cm x 35.5cm (14″ x 14″)
- Cushion pad to fit cover
- 2 square templates
- Fusible web with paper backing
- Thick, strong sewing thread
- Assorted 100% cotton patterned fabric remnants
- 9 assorted buttons

Equipment

- Needle
- Iron for pressing
- Pencil
- Ruler
- Fabric scissors and craft scissors

1 Draw around the templates onto the smooth side of the fusible web paper: 9 small squares and 9 large squares. Cut out the 18 squares.

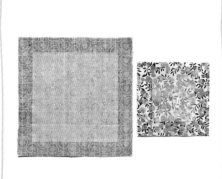

2 Iron the fusible web paper onto the reverse of assorted fabric pieces, with the paper's straight edge on the grain of the fabric.

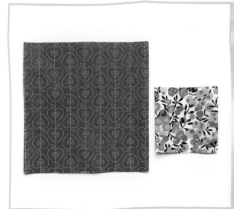

3 With fabric scissors, trim the fabric to the same size as the paper squares.

4 Remove the paper backing from the small fabric squares and, right sides up, iron them onto the centre of the large squares until they are fixed in place.

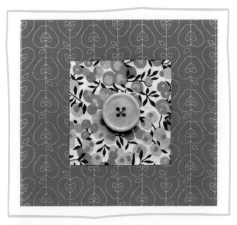

5 Place a button in the centre of the double square. Thread the needle and push it through the back of the fabric to come out through a hole in the button on top. Leave the thread loose at the back; don't knot it.

Make one stitch in each pair of holes. (If the button has only 2 holes, make 2 stitches.)

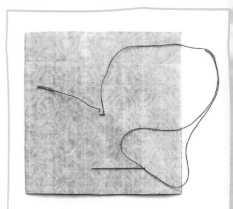

6 Turn the square over and remove the needle from the thread.

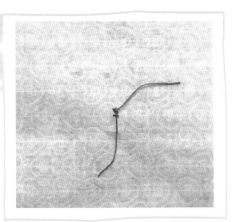

7 Make a tight knot with the loose ends of the thread. Trim the thread with scissors, but not too short. Repeat for all 9 patches.

Remove the backing paper from each one, tearing gently around the knot to prevent it coming untied.

8 With the zip at the bottom, place 3 patches in a row at the top edge of the cover. Iron in position, avoiding the buttons.

9 Repeat for the next line of 3 squares, continuing downwards until the cover is completed.

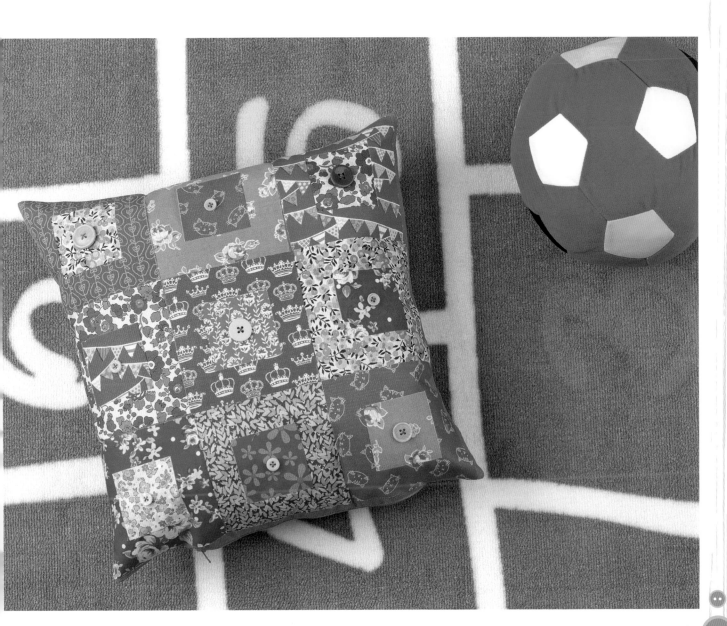

To make the cushion with triangular patches, you will need:

Materials

- 100% percale cotton zipped cushion cover 35.5cm x 35.5cm (14″ x 14″)
- Cushion pad to fit cover
- Star and triangle templates
- Fusible web with paper backing
- Assorted 100% cotton fabric remnants
- Optional: sheet of printer paper, if you don't have a quilting ruler

Equipment

- Iron for pressing
- Pencil
- Ruler
- Fabric scissors and craft scissors
- Optional: quilting ruler

1 Draw around the star template 8 times onto the smooth side of the fusible web paper.

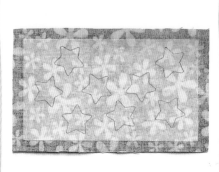

2 Choose a fabric that contrasts with the other colours used. Iron the web paper, smooth side upwards, onto the reverse side of the fabric.

3 Cut out the stars with fabric scissors and remove the backing paper.

4 Draw around the patchwork templates onto web paper, as before: 8 large triangles and 4 small triangles. Iron onto the reverse of assorted fabrics and cut out. Remove the backing papers.

Use a quilting ruler to help you position a large triangle's long side at right angles to the cushion case top, half way along. Alternatively, use a corner and 2 edges of a sheet of paper to do the same thing.

Iron in place. Put the long side of another triangle next to it, and press down with the iron.

Iron a star in the middle of each triangular patch.

5 Iron the other rectangles in place as shown, and add stars to all the larger patches.

6 Insert a pad into each finished cushion.

POCKET

Prehistorics and Pets

Hand stitch some soft-touch creatures to play with and display in pockets.

TIP Keep checking with a ruler that the seams aren't becoming wobbly, and aim to sew the back of the animal as neatly as the front.

Materials

- Pocket template
- 3 prehistoric animal templates
- Heavyweight iron-on interfacing cut to a 30cm x 44cm (12″ x 17″) rectangle
- 100% cotton fabric in 2 contrasting designs
- Felt fabric in 3 colours
- Bias binding 25mm (1″) wide
- Fusible web with paper backing
- 6 mini buttons
- Polyester filling or stuffing fibre
- Sewing thread
- Embroidery floss / thread
- Trouser hanger

Equipment

- Sewing machine, threaded
- Pencil
- Ruler
- Pinking shears
- Pins
- Needle
- Fabric scissors and craft scissors
- Iron for pressing

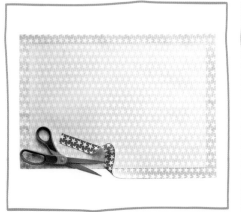

1 Iron the interfacing onto the reverse side of the main fabric, following the grain, until fixed in place.

Trim the fabric to the same size as the interfacing.

2 Draw around the pocket template onto the fusible web paper's smooth side, 3 times. Cut about 1cm (.4″) outside the pencil outline. Iron the 3 pocket shapes onto the reverse of the second fabric.

3 With pinking shears, cut the sides and bottom of the pocket on the outside of the pencil line. Cut the pocket top with fabric scissors.

4 Cut bias binding strips wider than the pockets. Iron paper-backed fusible web onto the reverse of each strip.

5 Fold the bias binding in half lengthways, and make a crease in it with your fingers. Remove the web's backing paper and pin the folded binding on top of the pocket. Iron in place and remove the pins.

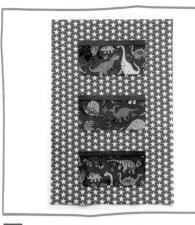

6 Trim off the excess pocket binding with pinking shears.

Pin the pockets to the centre of the backing fabric with 5cm (2″) between each one. Machine stitch the sides and bottom of the pockets, .5cm (.2″) from the edge. Machine stitch all the way round the backing fabric, also .5cm (.2″) from the edge.

7 Fold a piece of felt and place an animal template on it. Pin the felt close to the template, and draw around the template with a pencil. Transfer the pins onto the animal, and cut it out on the inside of the pencil line.

8 With sewing thread, hand stitch a button to each side of the animal's head.

If your embroidery thread contains 6 strands, separate them and use 3 strands to hand sew the sides of the animal together with running stitches.

When about half of the sewing is completed, start to lightly fill with stuffing fibre. Continue to fill in small amounts until the animal is stitched together.

9 Repeat for the other 2 animals.

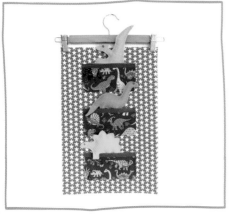

10 Pink the edges of the backing panel, keeping clear of the machine stitching. Suspend the panel from a trouser hanger and place the animals in pockets.

11 To change to pocket pets instead, make the backing panel in exactly the same way with different fabrics.

12 Use the rabbit template to make new animals.

13 Another beautiful addition to your space.

SPOTTED

Gift Wraps

A round stamp made from an eraser can be used
in a variety of gift wrap options.

TIP If you don't have an apple corer to press out the stamp, you can still
stick shapes onto a wrapped present. The stamped centres can be replaced
with coloured round sticky labels.

Materials

- A roll of ribbed brown parcel paper
- White plastic eraser
- Turquoise ribbon and white ribbon, both 15mm (.6″) wide
- Blank gift tags: 2 brown and 2 white
- Double sided clear adhesive tape to wrap the gifts
- Fine cotton cord

Equipment

- Apple corer
- Small chopping board
- Turquoise stamp pad
- White stamp pad
- Scissors
- Hole punch

1 On a chopping board or other hard, flat surface, press the apple corer firmly into a plastic eraser to produce a round stamp.

2 Press the stamp onto the turquoise ink pad and print onto the brown paper once only. Repeat over the paper, inking the stamp each time you print.

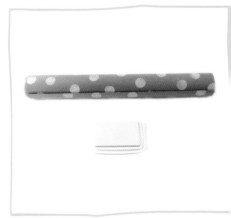

3 Clean the stamp. On a fresh roll of paper, print spots using the white ink pad.

Wrap your two gifts in different papers.

4 Punch holes randomly in the brown tag, and pair it with an unpunched white tag.

5 Do the same in reverse with another pair of brown and white tags.

6 Thread cotton cord through the tag tops, and knot it.

7 On the turquoise spotted parcel, tie a white ribbon with a knot leaving 2 loose ends. Slip the tag cord over one loose end before completing a bow.

Repeat with the white spotted paper and the turquoise ribbon.

Messages can be written on the plain under-tags.

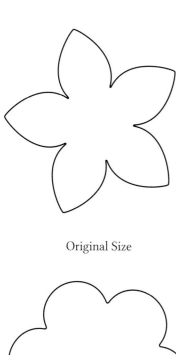

Original Size

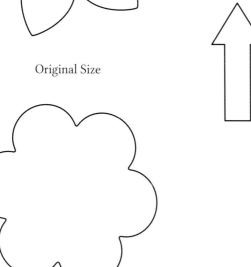

To make the
flowery
gift wrap,
you will need:

Materials

- A round stamp made from a plastic eraser (see above)
- A box wrapped in brown parcel paper
- Optional: 2 flower templates, if you are not using craft punches
- Optional: piece of card
- Assorted patterned fabrics
- A few sheets of good quality printer paper
- A plain white gift tag
- Glue stick

Equipment

- Optional: 2 large flower punches, or use templates and cut out the flowers by hand
- Stamp pads in 2 different colours
- Optional: scissors

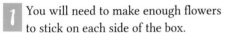

1 You will need to make enough flowers to stick on each side of the box.

2 Place 2 fabrics at a time on the photocopier's transparent plate, and colour photocopy onto sheets of good quality paper. Aim to produce 4 or 5 sheets of different copied fabrics.

Either stamp out flower shapes with craft punches, or draw around flower templates onto the photocopied sheets, and cut out.

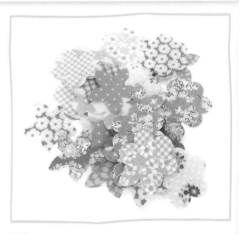

3 Check that there are enough flowers to cover all 6 sides of the box.

4 Use a round cut-out from a plastic eraser and coloured stamp pads to add a spot to the centre of each flower. Clean the stamp before changing to a different coloured pad.

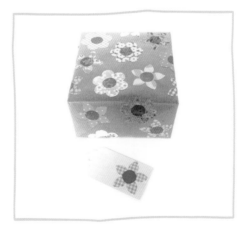

5 Glue each stamped flower onto the parcel, keeping one to decorate the white tag. Tie with ribbon if you wish.

Materials

- A box wrapped in brown parcel paper
- A round stamp made from a plastic eraser (see above)
- Arrow template
- Optional: 2 round templates 3.8cm (1.5″) diameter and 5cm (2″) diameter, if not using craft punches
- Colour photocopy of striped fabric
- Sheets of coloured paper
- Plain brown gift tag
- Glue stick

Equipment

- Optional: 2 round craft punches producing circles 3.8cm (1.5″) diameter and 5cm (2″) diameter, or use templates and cut the circles out by hand
- Scissors
- Stamp pads in 2 different colours
- Pencil
- Eraser

1 Draw around the arrow template onto the photocopy of striped fabric so that the stripes are at right angles to the long sides of the arrow. Repeat until you have enough arrows for 6 sides of the box.

Cut out, and erase any pencil marks showing.

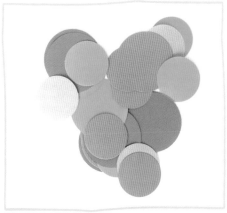

2 On coloured paper, either stamp out small and large circles with craft punches, or use the round templates and cut out the circles by hand. An equal number of large and small circles will be needed.

3 Glue the small circles onto the centres of the large ones.

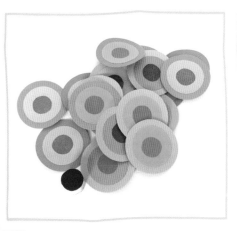

4 Use a round stamp and coloured ink pads to print a spot in the middle of each double circle.

5 Glue the circles and arrows onto the brown wrapping paper, and keep a circle in reserve to stick on the tag. Let the circle overlap the edge of the tag, and trim it off when the glue is dry Tie the gift with ribbon if you wish.

FLUTED
CARDBOARD TAGS

Make beautiful gift tags from pieces of waste cardboard.

TIP Ensure that the cardboard can be cut easily with scissors before you start, and practise with the hole punch on oddments first.

To make the heart tags, you will need:

Materials

- Brown cardboard with corrugated / fluted centre, 2mm (approx .1″) thick
- Card templates for 2 hearts and 2 heart-centres
- Glue stick
- 1 sheet good quality white printer paper
- Floral fabric remnant
- Bakers' twine
- Clear cellulose tape

Equipment

- Pencil
- Small hole punch or bradawl
- Scissors
- Pinking shears
- Colour photocopier

1 Place the bumpy side of the cardboard upwards. Draw around the large heart templates twice, then around the smaller heart templates twice.

Cut out the four hearts with scissors.

2 Either punch a small hole at the top of each heart in the centre, or pierce with a bradawl.

3 With the smoothest side of the cardboard on the outside, stick the hearts together to make one large and one small tag.

4 Colour photocopy your chosen fabric onto a sheet of good quality paper.

5 On the back of the paper, draw around the heart-centre templates twice each.

With pinking shears, cut on the outside of the pencil lines.

6 Stick the heart-centres on each side of the cardboard tags.

7 Wrap a small piece of clear sticky tape around one end of the bakers' twine to push it through the holes. Snip the tape off once the tags are threaded.

8 Cut a double length of twine 11cm (4.5″) for the larger tag and 19cm (7.5″) for the smaller tag. Knot them together as shown.

9 When tying a gift ribbon, add the tags before completing the bow.

Original Size

Original Size

Materials

- Brown cardboard with corrugated / fluted centre, 2mm (approx .1″) thick
- Large and small round-top tag templates
- Optional: large and small daisy templates, if you are not using craft punches
- Remnant of thin white card
- Remnant of thin green card
- 3 small yellow buttons with 2 holes
- 1 yellow mini button
- Yellow sewing thread
- Bakers' twine

Equipment

- Scissors
- Needle
- Pencil
- Pair of compasses
- Optional: large and small flower punches, or use templates and cut out the flowers by hand
- Small hole punch or bradawl

1 Use the tag templates to cut 2 large and 2 small brown cardboard shapes. Make a hole at the top of each one with either a hole punch or a bradawl.

On white card, either stamp out 3 large and 1 small flower with craft punches, or draw around the templates and cut them out by hand.

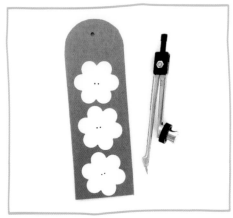

2 Glue the 3 bigger flowers on a large tag, as shown. Pierce two holes in the centre of each flower with a compass point.

3 With a needle and double thread, stitch a button onto each flower, through to the cardboard backing.

4 Glue the 2 sides of the large tag together.

5 Cut a piece of green card to cover most of the small tag on one side. Add a flower and sew on the small button.

Stick the back of the small tag in place, and thread both tags with bakers' twine.

6 Knot the twine so that the smaller tag shows just below the big one when hanging on the wrapped present.

Materials

- Brown cardboard with corrugated / fluted centre, 2mm (approx .1″) thick
- Oblong tag template
- Hat template
- Remnants of white card and red card
- Red emulsion paint
- White emulsion paint
- Small vinyl self-adhesive star labels
- Bakers' twine
- 2 small pompoms
- All-purpose or fabric glue
- Glue stick

Equipment

- Paintbrush
- Small hole punch or bradawl
- Scissors
- Pin

1 On the red and white card, stick stars over an area bigger than the hat template.

2 With a paintbrush, cover the stars on the red card with white paint. Paint over the stars on the white card in red. Allow to dry.

3 Use the pin to help lift the corners of the star labels to remove them.

4 Draw round the hat templates on each red and white combination, and cut out.

5 Cut 2 brown tags, pierce them and glue them together. Stick one hat above the other using the glue stick. Change to the all-purpose or fabric glue to fix the pompoms on top of the hats.

6 Thread with bakers' twine and hang from a gift.

Paper Collage
GREETINGS CARDS

Photocopy a selection of remnants, then cut out
the papers and stick onto card blanks.

TIP Experiment with a few fabrics beforehand, because some colours can
look disappointingly dull when printed onto paper.

To make a lace and flower card, you will need:

Materials

- White square blank card 13.5cm x 13.5cm (5" x 5")
- 1m (1 yd) lace trim with a wavy edge, 30mm (1.2") wide
- Good quality white printer paper
- Sheet of bright pink paper or card
- Floral fabric remnant
- Red spotted fabric remnant
- Pink patterned fabric remnant
- Glue stick
- Vase template
- Square template 9.5cm x 9.5cm (3.75" x 3/75")

Equipment

- Colour photocopier
- Scissors
- Pencil

1 Lay the lace trim across the copier's glass plate as 2 strips.

2 Place the pink paper or card on top of the lace.

3 Close the copier lid and colour photocopy onto good quality printer paper.

4 Cut the strips away from the background just outside the edge of the lace. Cut in half again to make 4 short lace strips.

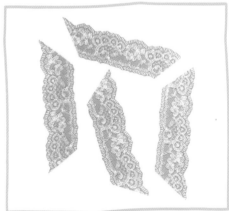

5 Trim the lace so that each wavy edge is the same length as the sides of the card. Cut the lace ends at an angle to make mitred corners when you stick them on the card.

6 Glue the lace onto the card so that it resembles a picture frame.

7 Photocopy the floral fabric and the pink patterned fabric onto the same sheet of paper.

8 Draw around the vase template onto the back of the pink photocopy, and cut out.

9 Select motifs from the floral photocopy to position onto the vase, and on the corners of the lace. Cut them out.

10 On the back of a red fabric photocopy, draw around the square template.

11 Cut out along the pencil line, and stick onto the card centrally.

12 Stick down the vase, and add a group of flowers on top as though the vase contains a bouquet. Glue a single flower at each corner of the lace.

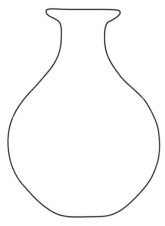

Original Size

Materials

- Brown square blank card 13.5cm x 13.5cm (5" x 5")
- Photocopies of floral fabric in 2 different designs
- Sheet of brown kraft paper
- Mini button
- Sewing thread
- Rabbit template

Equipment

- Scissors
- Needle
- Pencil
- Pair of compasses

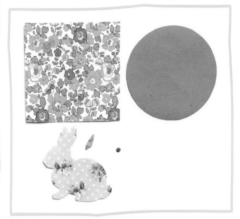

1 Cut a fabric photocopy to fit the front of the blank greetings card.

With compasses, draw a circle on brown paper slightly smaller than the card front, and cut out.

Draw around the rabbit template onto a different fabric photocopy, and cut out. Cut up the rabbit's ear to obtain the template for its inner shape. Use this small template on the first fabric.

2 Glue the fabric background in place on the right-hand side of the card before folding it.

3 Stick the brown circle in the centre of the card.

4 Glue the rabbit onto the brown circle, and stick on its inner ear.

5 From the template, mark the position of the eye lightly in pencil. Insert thread into the needle and pull it so that it's double. Knot the ends of the thread together. Push the needle through the card from inside, to come out at the eye. Thread the needle through the holes in the button.

6 Make 2 or 3 stitches through the card to hold the button in place. Return the needle to the inside of the card.

7 Knot the thread close to the card and snip of the ends with scissors.

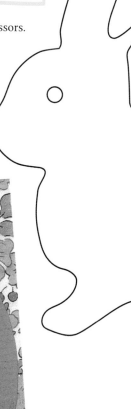

Original Size

To make a rocket card, you will need:

Materials

- Brown square blank card 13.5cm x 13.5cm (5" x 5")
- Photocopy of starry sky fabric (or find a photo of outer space online, and print it onto paper)
- Photocopies of 4 different fabric remnants: orange, yellow, striped and spotted
- Glue stick
- Rocket template
- Square template 11.5cm x 11.5cm (4.5" x 4.5")

Equipment

- Pinking shears
- Pencil
- Scissors

1 Fold the blank card along the central crease.

2 Draw around the square template onto the back of the outer space printed image. With pinking shears, cut on the outside of the pencil line.

3 Positioning centrally, glue onto the card front.

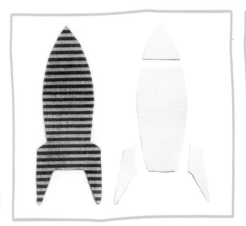

4 Draw round the whole rocket template on the striped photocopy, and cut it out.

Cut the template's internal lines and separate the nose-cone and fins from the rest of the rocket.

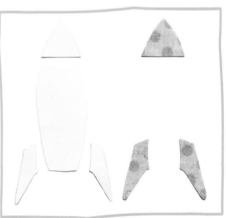

5 Use the nose-cone and fins templates to cut shapes from the spotted photocopy.

6 Draw around the whole flame onto the yellow paper. Cut the template, and draw around the flame centre on the orange paper.

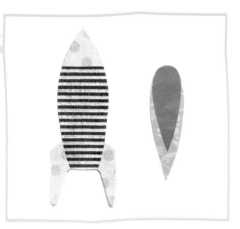

7 Glue the nose-cone and fins on the striped rocket. Glue the orange part of the flame onto the yellow part.

8 Stick the rocket and the flame onto the card diagonally to complete it.

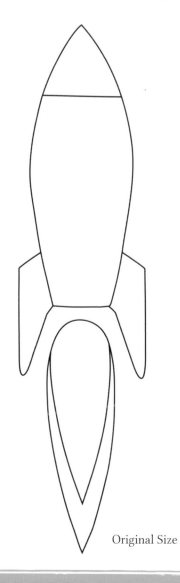

Original Size

FaBRiC FaCeD

CLOCK

Create a unique clock by selecting your favourite
fabric and adding inexpensive components.

TIP It's a good idea to make sure the stick-on numbers can be seen clearly
against your choice of patterned background.

To make a clock, you will need:

Materials

- 25cm (10″) diameter wooden disc with central hole
- 100% cotton patterned fabric 50cm x 55cm (20″ x 21.5″)
- Vinyl self-adhesive numbers, 15mm (.6″) high
- PVA glue
- Quartz clock mechanism with integral hook for hanging, and battery

Equipment

- Pencil
- Ruler
- Pair of compasses
- Fabric scissors
- Small decorators' paintbrush
- Cup or bowl

1 Measure the clock's diameter exactly. On paper or card, draw a circle that has a diameter slightly smaller than the clock. Cut out.

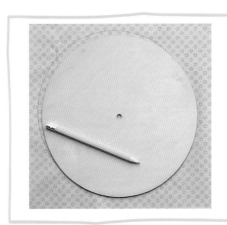

2 With a pencil, draw round the paper or card template onto the reverse side of the fabric. Cut out.

Also, draw round the wooden disc onto a different part of the fabric. With the help of a ruler, make pencil marks 4cm (1.6″) from the edge of this outline, to make a bigger circle outside the first one. Cut along the outside circle.

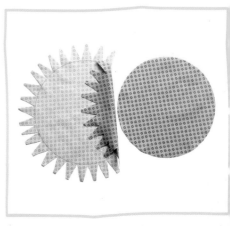

3 In the larger fabric piece, cut a series of 'V' shapes between the inside and outside circle.

4 Apply PVA glue to one side of the wooden disc with a paintbrush.

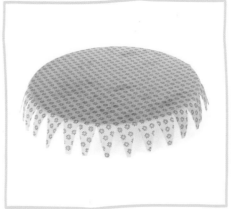

5 Position the larger fabric piece right side up onto the disc, and smooth it down. Place onto a cup or bowl to dry.

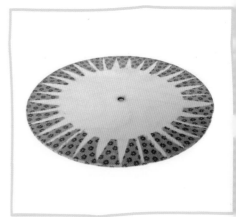

6 Turn the disc over and glue the fabric edges to the wood. Ensure the fabric fits the rim snugly, smoothing with fingers if necessary. Leave to dry.

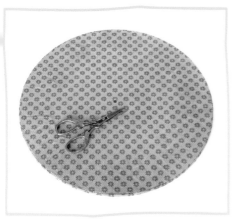

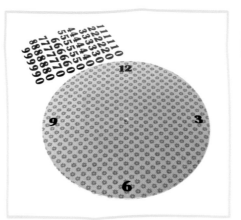

7 Apply glue all over the back and place the smaller fabric circle on it, smoothing it down. When dry, add a further layer of glue on top of the fabric at the back, and then at the front.

Once dry again, snip the fabric on both sides to reveal the hole in the wood.

8 Stick on the self-adhesive numbers, starting with 3, 6, 9 and 12.

9 Add the numbers in between, equally spaced.

10 Dab glue gently on top of the numbers. Don't pull the brush across them in case the colour runs slightly. When dry, coat the clock face with a final layer of glue.

11 Insert the clock mechanism according to the manufacturer's instructions. Position the integral hook at the top, ready to hang.

12 Put in the battery, and adjust to the correct time.

FLOWER GARLAND

A lovely floral ring from fabric scraps, but without any stitching or gluing.

TIP Use good quality tissue paper that won't disintegrate when you brush it onto the polystyrene shape.

Materials

- 20cm (8″) rounded, flat-backed polystyrene wreath
- Light green tissue paper
- PVA glue
- Flower templates
- Heavyweight iron-on interfacing
- Remnants of yellow felt and 100% cotton patterned yellow fabric in two different designs
- 15 x yellow and orange round wooden beads, 12mm (.5″)
- 15 x yellow, natural and orange tube wooden beads, 12mm x 6mm (.5″ x .25″)
- 30 yellow and orange glass-headed dressmaking pins 30mm - 43mm long (1.2″ - 1.7″)
- 15cm (6″) gingham ribbon, 10mm (.4″) wide
- 2 x strong double-sided sticky pads

Equipment

- Small decorators' paintbrush
- Cereal bowl approximately the same size as the wreath
- Pencil
- Iron for pressing
- Fabric scissors and craft scissors

1 Tear up enough green tissue paper into postage stamp sized pieces to loosely fill the cereal bowl.

Brush PVA glue onto an area of the polystyrene wreath. Place some tissue pieces over this area, overlapping slightly. Brush more glue on the top, keeping the tissue flat and as free from wrinkles as possible. Repeat until the back and front of the wreath are covered. Allow to dry by balancing on the rim of the cereal bowl.

Apply a second layer of tissue paper. When dry, paint a final coat of glue all over.

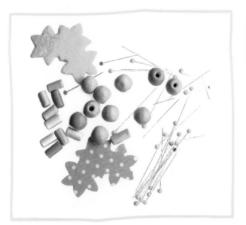

3 Cut out the flower shapes with fabric scissors. Assemble the pins and beads ready for attaching the flowers to the wreath.

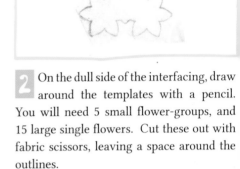

2 On the dull side of the interfacing, draw around the templates with a pencil. You will need 5 small flower-groups, and 15 large single flowers. Cut these out with fabric scissors, leaving a space around the outlines.

Shiny side down, iron these onto the wrong sides of the yellow fabric pieces with an iron. Do roughly the same number of flower shapes from each of the three fabrics. Allow to cool and check that the fabric is completely fused to the interfacing.

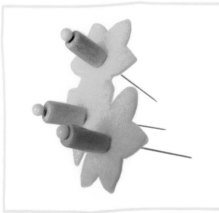

4 Start by positioning the 5 flower-groups on the top surface of the wreath, with equal distances between them. Select three wooden tube beads of the same colour for each flower group motif. Select the most suitable (closest) pin colour for your chosen tube beads.

6 On the back, attach two sticky pads, one under the other. Press on the gingham ribbon so that all the adhesive is covered. The garland is now ready to hang.

5 Push the pins through the beads, fabric and polystyrene to fix the flowers in place. Check that the pin is embedded and not poking through the other side of the wreath.

Position three single flowers between each flower-group as shown, topped by the round beads this time. These flowers will be at a slight angle, using spaces at the sides of the wreath rather than directly on top. Distribute the fabric and bead colours to give you a balanced, varied result.

Original Size

Recycled

MINI VASES

A new way of upcycling glass jars to decorate your space.

TIP Although the finished surface will wipe clean, avoid getting water where the paint ends, and the glass begins.

For the set of 4 posy pots, you will need:

▶ Materials ◀

- ☑ 4 small empty glass jars, e.g. spice containers
- ☑ White gesso acrylic primer
- ☑ 4 tubes of thick acrylic paint in pastel colours (runny paint won't produce good coverage)
- ☑ 3 metres (3 yards) thin cotton cord
- ☑ Good quality masking tape

▶ Equipment ◀

- ☑ Small decorators' paintbrush
- ☑ Optional: artists' sable brush for the acrylic colours
- ☑ Scissors

1 Remove the jar tops. Add washing up liquid to warm water, then clean out any residue and soak off the labels.

2 Pour an equal amount of clean water into each jar, about halfway up.

3 Wrap a strip of masking tape around each jar. The bottom of the tape should be on the water level.

4 Once taped, tip out the water and dab the exterior dry.

5 Invert the jars and paint a coat of acrylic primer on the bottom half. Allow several hours to dry.

6 Paint on a second coat of primer, and a third if necessary, until the glass is evenly covered.

7 Apply two coats of coloured acrylic paint to a jar.

8 Repeat with the other jars. As with the primer, ensure each coat of paint dries thoroughly.

9 Remove the masking tape.

10 Once removed, the jar is ready for the cord to be added.

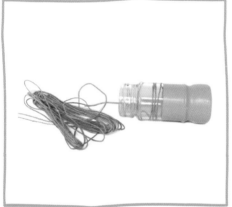

11 Hold one end of the cord against the middle of the jar, and wrap the cord around the clear glass five times.

12 Push the rows of cord together down to the painted area. Knot the ends together tightly and snip off the excess cord. For best effect, display the vases in the same order as the colours of a rainbow, and add similar flower posies to each one.

To make a butterfly vase for dry flowers, or a pencil pot, you will need:

Materials

- Empty glass jar
- White gesso acrylic primer
- 2 x A4 (8.5″ x 11″) thin white card
- Lace fabric
- Permanent glue dots
- 4 sheets coloured paper
- Optional: butterfly template, if you are not using a craft punch

Equipment

- Computer printer or photocopier
- Small decorators' paintbrush
- Optional: large butterfly punch, or use a template and cut out the butterflies by hand
- Optional: pencil
- Optional: scissors

1 Brush a coat of primer on the outside of the jar. Allow to dry thoroughly. Add 4 or 5 more coats until the jar surface is evenly covered, leaving to dry in between.

2 Lay the lace fabric across the copier's glass plate.

3 Place 2 sheets of coloured paper side by side on top of the lace, and close the copier lid.

Photocopy onto each side of a sheet of white card. Repeat with 2 different coloured papers.

4 Either punch out several butterflies in different card colours, or draw around the butterfly template and cut them out.

5 Make 2 folds in each butterfly either side of its central body.

6 Place a glue dot on the centre of the butterfly's underside, and press it firmly onto the jar.

8 Add further butterflies to complete the project.

Original Size

To make a decoupage posy pot for dry flowers, you will need:

Materials

- Empty glass jar
- White gesso acrylic primer
- Thick acrylic paint in a pale colour
- 1 or 2 floral paper serviettes (napkins)
- PVA glue

Equipment

- Small decorators' paintbrush
- Fine artists' paintbrush
- Tumbler containing water

1 Brush on 2 coats of gesso primer followed by 3 coats of acrylic paint. Allow to dry thoroughly in between.

2 Peel the top printed layer from the serviette.

3 Dip the fine paintbrush in the water and paint a wet circle on the paper around a flower motif. The motif should then push through easily from the surrounding dry paper. Repeat until you have enough flowers for the outside of the jar.

4 Paint PVA glue on a motif-sized area of the jar surface. Apply the flower motif to the sticky surface and brush its edges down until flat. Avoid brushing the printed flower in case the colour runs.

5 When the jar surface is dry, dab glue on top of each flower. When dry again, varnish the rest of the jar's exterior with longer brushstrokes of glue.

BUNTING

Make bunting quickly by backing thin card with self-adhesive craft foam.

TIP Use twine manufactured from natural fibre, otherwise it will be too slippery to hold the flags in position.

▶ Materials ◀

▱ Fabric remnant with pattern against a white/cream background

▱ 4-5 sheets A4 (8.5″ x 11″) brown ribbed kraft paper

▱ White plastic eraser

▱ Flag template

▱ 4-5 red self-adhesive foam sheets, A4 size (8.5″ x 11″)

▱ Cotton bakers' twine, red and white striped

▶ Equipment ◀

▱ Apple corer

▱ Red stamp pad

▱ Photocopier

▱ Pencil

▱ Scissors

▱ Single hole punch

1 Unfold the fabric and lay it face down on the glass plate of the photocopier.

Press the button for a black and white photocopy, and print out onto two sheets of brown kraft paper. Put to one side for now.

2 To make a round decorative stamp, press an apple corer into a plastic eraser.

3 Ink the stamp, and apply to a sheet of brown paper once. Re-ink and repeat until there are multiple spots on the paper. Print a further sheet of brown paper in the same way.

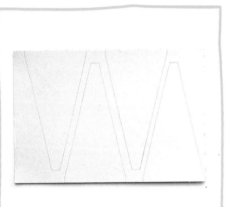

4 Draw around the flag template onto the backing paper of the foam sheet as many times as possible. Cut out these shapes.

5 Peel off the white paper from half of the shapes to reveal the sticky surface.

6 Stick onto the reverse of the photocopied paper. Trim the patterned paper so that it's the same size as the red foam backing.

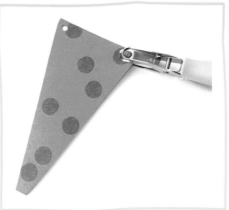

8 With a hole punch, perforate each side of the flag tops. Ensure the punch is not too close to the edge of the flag; practise on some waste paper first.

7 Do the same again, using the spotted paper this time. Repeat until you have 8 spotted flags and 8 patterned flags.

9 Arrange the bunting in a row, alternating patterned and spotted flags. Leaving a 20 – 30 cm (8″ – 12″) knotted 'tail' at each end, thread with bakers' twine to complete the bunting. Arrange the twine so that most of it lies at the back of the flags.

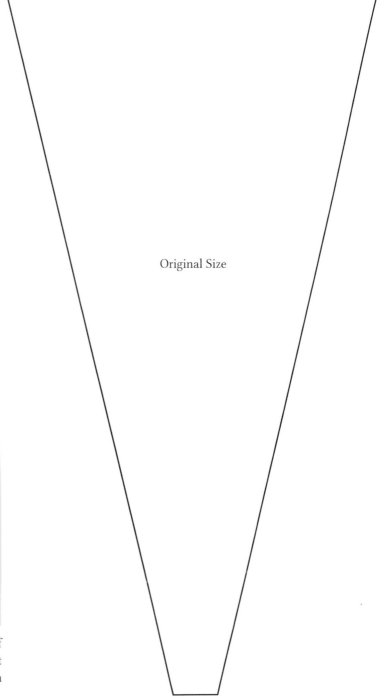

Original Size

10 No further knotting is required; the combination of the slightly textured cotton twine and the lightweight foam should enable the flags maintain their position when hung up.

Materials

- White plastic eraser
- 4-5 red self-adhesive foam sheets, A4 size (8.5″ x 11″)
- Card in assorted bright colours
- Cotton bakers' twine, striped
- Self-adhesive star label
- Swallow-tailed flag template
- Optional: star template, if you are not using a craft punch
- Glue stick

Equipment

- Pencil
- Ink pads in different colours
- Craft knife (adult help advised)
- Small chopping board
- Scissors
- Single hole punch
- Optional: large star craft punch, or draw round a template and cut by hand

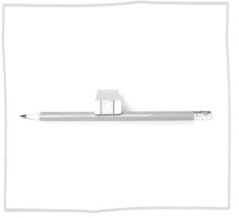

1 With a pencil, mark a square shape on the end of the eraser, using its whole thickness.

2 Stick a star label at the other end of the eraser, on its widest side. Mark a cutting line near to the star.

3 On the chopping board, cut off the area containing the star with a craft knife. Cut the sides of the square down the remaining length of the eraser.

4 With the knife blade against the sides of the star, chop downwards to remove the surrounding plastic.

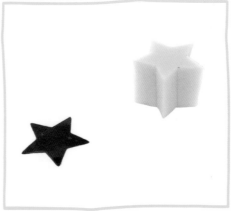

5 When just the star-shaped plastic is left, remove the sticky label.

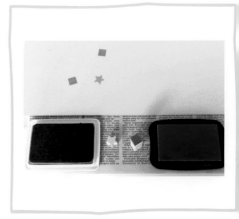

6 Use the star and square stamps to print coloured ink shapes onto the card.

7 Cut bunting flags from the foam sheets using the template, as before (see above).

Stick half of the foam flags onto the back of the stamped card, and cut out.

8 Make an equal number of plain flags from unstamped coloured card.

Either press out some star shapes with a star punch, or draw around the star template onto coloured card and cut out by hand.

9 Glue the cut-out stars onto the plain flags. Punch 2 holes in each flag. Thread them with bakers' twine, alternating stamped and unstamped bunting.

Original Size

Materials

- 4-5 red self-adhesive foam sheets, A4 size (8.5" x 11")
- Jumper template
- Card in assorted bright colours
- Several photocopies of patterned fabric on good quality printer paper
- Cotton bakers' twine, striped
- Glue stick

Equipment

- Pencil
- Ruler
- Scissors
- Single hole punch

To make jumper-shaped bunting, you will need:

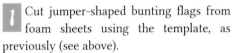

1 Cut jumper-shaped bunting flags from foam sheets using the template, as previously (see above).

Peel the backing paper from half of the flags and stick them onto the reverse of the fabric photocopies. Cut off the excess paper with scissors.

2 Stick the other half of the foam shapes onto coloured card, and cut out.

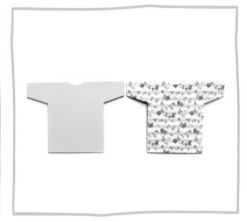

3 Make several bunting flags in this way. Some jumpers will be plain card and other jumpers will be patterned.

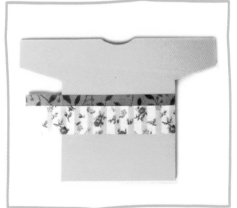

4 On the plain flags, cut 2 strips of photocopied fabric wider than the body of the jumper. Glue them in place. Trim off the excess paper.

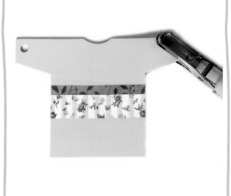

5 Perforate the ends of the sleeves with the hole punch.

6 String the flags onto twine, alternating striped and patterned jumpers.

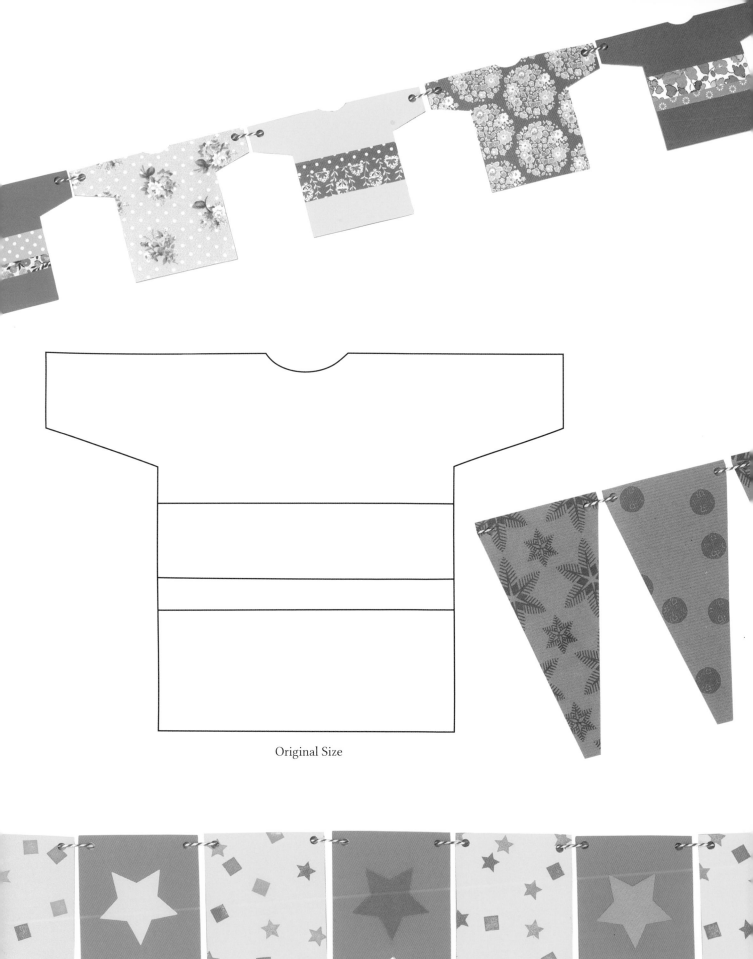

Original Size

UNIQUE TREES

Build a weird and wonderful tree, and then clip on some unusual 'fruit'.

TIP You may be more likely to find suitable twigs at the local florist shop than by hunting around your neighbourhood or looking online.

To make a sweetheart tree, you will need:

Materials

- Terracotta flower pot
- Green emulsion paint
- Turquoise emulsion paint
- Florists' foam
- Dried twigs
- 3 sheets of mauve paper
- Recycled brown cardboard that can be cut easily with scissors
- Assortment of coloured card (red, orange, yellow, beige, pale pink, deep pink, bright blue, light green)
- Tree decoration templates
- Wooden mini clothes pegs, 5cm (2") long
- All-purpose glue for the clothes pegs
- Glue stick for the card

Equipment

- Kitchen knife
- Chopping board
- Small decorators' paintbrush
- Scissors
- Pinking shears

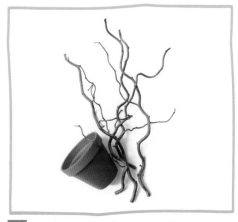

1 Wash out the flowerpot if necessary, and trim the twigs to a similar length.

2 Paint 2 coats of green emulsion on the outside of the pot.

3 Paint the inside where it will be seen in the finished project.

4 With a kitchen knife, cut up a block of florists' foam to fit in the flowerpot.

5 Push the foam in for a tight fit.

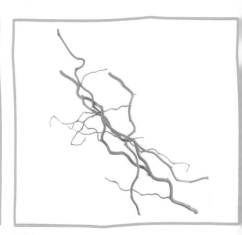

6 Paint the twigs with a coat of turquoise emulsion.

7 Push and twist the twigs into the foam until they are firmly in place.

8 Holding the 3 sheets of mauve paper together, cut into narrow strips. Roll the strips loosely between your palms.

9 Place the shredded paper around the base of the twigs to cover the foam.

10 Draw around each template onto the brown card, and cut out.

11 On the lolly shape, stick strips of red, orange, yellow and beige card, as shown.

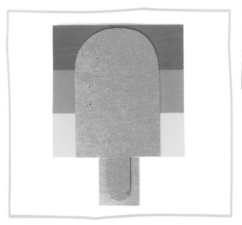

12 This will be the view from the back.

13 Use the template to cut a heart from light pink card. Stick onto the deep pink card.

14 Cut the deep pink card around the heart with pinking shears.

15 Cut the cake template to separate the top from the bottom. Draw around the top onto pink card, and cut out. Use the bottom of the template to cut the yellow card shape.

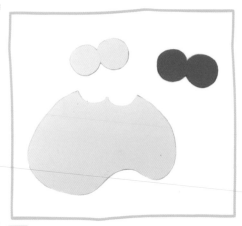

16 Cut the template again to separate the cherry shapes. Draw onto red card and cut out.

17 Cut up the ice cream template into 2 scoops and the cone, and use to produce the coloured card shapes. Cut out the blue dripping syrup last.

18 Trim the excess card from the lolly shape.

Glue the pink and yellow card on the cupcake shape, and stick the cherries on top of the pink icing.

Glue the ice cream pieces together in the same way.

19 Turn the shapes over and use all-purpose glue to stick the pegs to the back of them. Avoid sticking the pegs on too high up, otherwise they will be visible from the front.

20 Peg the decorations onto the twigs. Make as many more decorations as you need to fill your tree.

Materials

☑ Recycled brown cardboard that can be cut easily with scissors
☑ 2 kite templates
☑ Narrow ribbon in 3 colours
☑ Blue and purple card
☑ Good quality printer paper
☑ Patterned fabric
☑ Glue stick for the card pieces
☑ All-purpose glue for the pegs
☑ Clear adhesive tape
☑ Wooden mini clothes pegs, 5cm (2") long

Equipment

☑ Photocopier
☑ Scissors
☑ Pencil

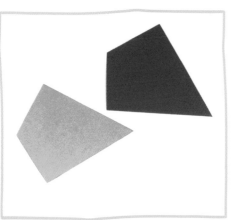

1 Use the large kite template to cut the brown base and the purple top.

2 Cut 3 ribbons to a length of about 15cm (6") each. Apply glue to the bottom of the brown card's reverse side. Stick on the first ribbon. Add more glue on top before sticking down the other two ribbons.

3 When dry, tape the ribbons down as well.

4 Colour photocopy some patterned fabric onto a sheet of good quality printer paper.

Cut up the kite template into 4 sections. Draw around a small and a large section onto the back of the photocopy.

5 Cut out the 2 pieces.

6 Stick onto the purple kite shape. With the ribbon inside, stick the kite front to the brown cardboard backing.

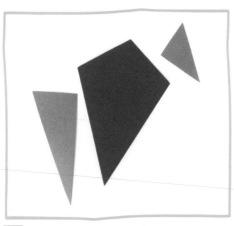
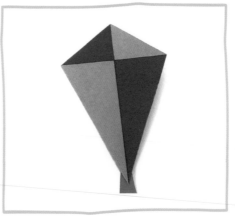

7 Use the other template to make a smaller kite, with plain blue sections on the front this time.

8 Complete the kite in the same way as before, but with 2 ribbons instead of 3. Cut the ribbons for the small kite to a length of 20cm (8").

9 With all-purpose glue, attach a peg to the widest part of each kite.

10 Peg the kites to the tree so that the ribbons can hang down freely.

Original Size

KEEPSAKE BOX

Stain an unvarnished box faster than painting it, and
add some of your favourite fabric to finish it off.

TIP To prevent the glue for the fabric discolouring the wood stain, stick
masking tape around the sides of the lid before varnishing the top.

To make a
keepsake box,
you will need:

Materials

- Unvarnished solid wood box
- Solvent-free, odourless interior wood stain (protective clothing advised)
- 100% cotton fabric, patterned
- Rectangular template 11cm x 15cm (4.5″ x 6″)
- 2 x 18cm (7″) cotton tapes, 10mm (.4″) wide
- Decoupage glue
- Old newspapers to protect surfaces

Equipment

- Small decorators' paintbrush
- Pencil
- Ruler
- Pinking shears
- Sewing machine and thread
- A few pins

1 Apply a single coat of stain with a paintbrush.

2 Paint only the edges of the lid top, about 1cm (.4″) wide.

3 Stain the inside as well as the outside. Allow to dry.

4 Measure the box lid. Using a pencil and ruler, draw a rectangle on the reverse of the fabric that is 1cm (.4″) shorter in length and 1cm (.4″) shorter in width than the lid.

Cut with pinking shears on the outside of the pencil line.

5 Brush decoupage glue on the top of the lid only.

6 Position the fabric, right side up, centrally on the box lid and leave to dry. When dry, brush another coat of decoupage glue on top of the fabric to complete the box.

7 To make a pouch for inside the box, draw around the rectangular template twice on the reverse of the fabric. Cut with pinking shears on the outside of the pencil lines.

8 Place the ends of the tape at each side of one fabric rectangle, face up. Put the other rectangle on top, face down. Pin the fabric and tape in place.

9 Machine 3 sides of the pouch, sewing the ends of the tape into the seams. Snip off the bottom corners of the pouch, staying clear of the stitching.

10 Turn inside out. Wrap the tapes around the neck of the pouch and tie in a bow.

11 The pouch can be kept inside the keepsake box to store small items, or extra-special belongings.

12 By using a different stain colour and fabric design, the box can be adapted to individual preferences.

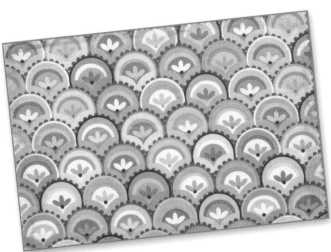

STASH BAGS

Personalise inexpensive cotton bags in a variety of ways using oddments.

TIP Some bags have been treated with a product that sticks to the iron; to avoid this, press through a damp tea towel to get rid of creases before you start, and use a sheet of kitchen paper roll when ironing over smaller areas.

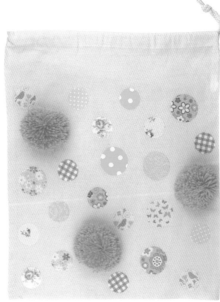

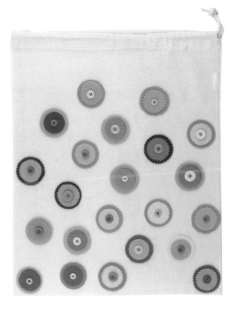

To make a bird bag, you will need:

Materials

⬧ Cotton drawstring bag 50cm x 75cm (20″ x 30″), pressed
⬧ Bird template
⬧ Fusible web with paper backing
⬧ 100% cotton assorted patterned fabric remnants

Equipment

⬧ Pencil
⬧ Fabric scissors and craft scissors
⬧ Iron for pressing

1 Draw around the template onto the smooth side of the web paper about 15 times, leaving gaps in between the birds. Cut around the birds, not on the outlines.

2 With the paper's smooth side upwards, iron the birds onto the reverse of different fabrics.

3 Cut out the birds with fabric scissors and remove the backing papers.

Original Size

4 Arrange the birds on the bag, right sides up, until you are pleased with the design. Iron on one bird at a time to fuse it to the bag.

To make a spotted bag, you will need:

Materials

- Cotton drawstring bag 50cm x 75cm (20″ x 30″), pressed
- Round template 5cm (2″) diameter
- Round template 3.8cm (1.5″) diameter
- Fusible web with paper backing
- 100% cotton assorted patterned fabric remnants
- Ball of knitting yarn

Equipment

- Pompom maker
- Pencil
- Iron for pressing
- Fabric scissors and craft scissors
- Large needle

1 Use a pompom maker following the manufacturer's instructions to produce a few pompoms. When tying them, leave the ends of the yarn uncut.

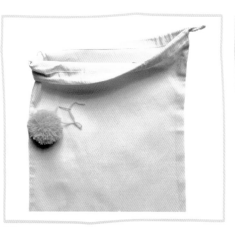

2 Thread the needle with a yarn end, and push the needle through the bag to the inside. Thread the needle again with the other yarn end, taking it through the bag near to the first yarn with a little fabric in between.

3 Knot the yarn ends inside the bag and trim with scissors.

4 Draw around the templates several times onto the smooth side of the fusible web paper. Leave space in between the circles.

5 Cut around the circles, not on the pencil outlines. Iron onto the reverse of assorted fabrics. When cool, cut out the circles with fabric scissors and remove the backing papers.

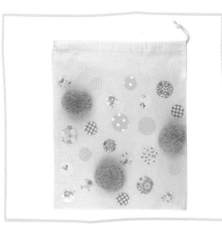

6 Iron the fabric shapes onto the bag in between the pompoms.

To make a button bag, you will need:

Materials

- Felt fabric remnants in assorted colours
- Cotton drawstring bag 50cm x 75cm (20″ x 30″), pressed
- Round template 5cm (2″) diameter
- Round template 3.8cm (1.5″) diameter
- Fusible web with paper backing
- Assorted buttons
- Strong, thick sewing thread
- Sheet of paper kitchen roll
- Permanent glue dots

Equipment

- Pinking shears
- Fabric scissors and craft scissors
- Pencil
- Iron for pressing
- Needle

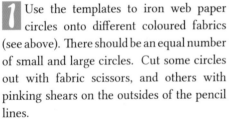

1 Use the templates to iron web paper circles onto different coloured fabrics (see above). There should be an equal number of small and large circles. Cut some circles out with fabric scissors, and others with pinking shears on the outsides of the pencil lines.

2 Remove the backing paper from the small circles. Place them on the large circles, and cover with the paper sheet before fusing them together with the iron.

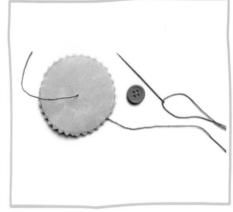

3 Thread the needle and push it through the felt circles to the front, leaving a short length of thread at the back.

4 Place a button on the small circle and make a stitch in each pair of holes (or 2 stitches if the button has only 2 holes).

5 Tie the 2 ends of thread together in a knot.

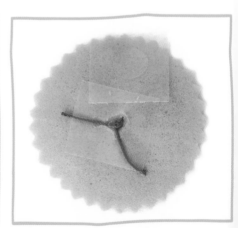

6 Remove the backing paper and stick 2 or more glue dots on the reverse of each large circle.

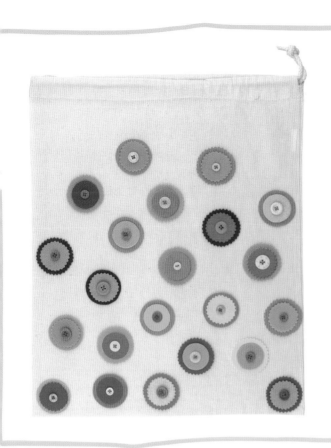

7 Press the circles in place on the bag.

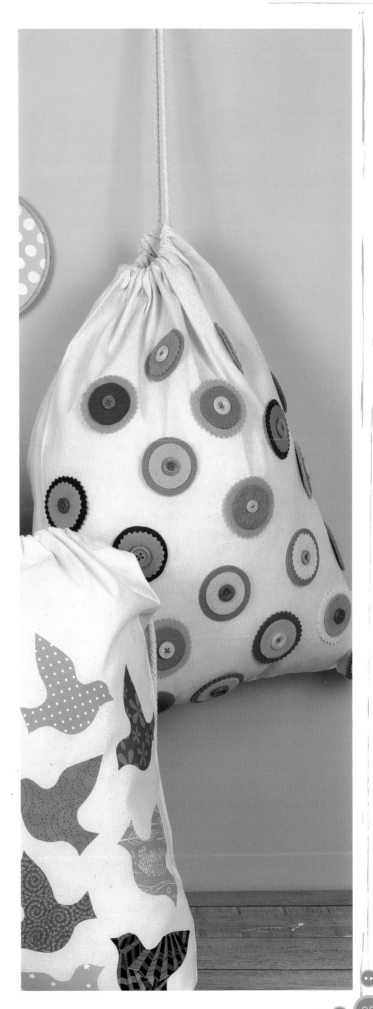

TREASURE TINS

Decorate candle-making containers to store your treasures.

TIP For beginners, an alternative to decorating with cotton fabric is to photocopy the fabric onto good quality office paper, and attach the paper using a glue stick rather than an adhesive sheet.

To customise a tin with patterned fabric, you will need:

Materials

- Double-sided adhesive sheet
- 100% cotton patterned fabric
- 250ml (8oz) candle making tin with lid
- 60cm (24") ribbon, 5mm (.2") wide
- Felt fabric remnant
- Sheet of graph paper or printer paper
- Double-sided clear adhesive tape

Equipment

- Pair of compasses with pencil
- Pinking shears
- Fabric scissors and craft scissors

1 On a double-sided adhesive sheet, draw 2 circles slightly smaller than the tin lid circumference, with compasses and a pencil. Cut out.

2 Peel off the backing paper from one side of the cut-out circles. Press the sticky side of the circles onto the reverse of the fabric.

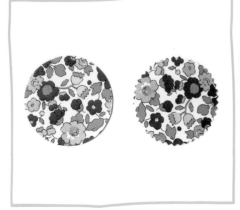

3 With fabric scissors, cut out both round shapes. With pinking shears, cut just inside the edge of one round shape only.

4 Taking the fabric circle with a smooth edge, peel off the remaining backing paper. Stick inside the lid.

5 Cut a piece of paper so that it fits around the tin, with a small overlap. This is easier with graph paper. Use the paper as a template to cut a rectangle from the adhesive sheet.

Stick the rectangle on the fabric as before, and cut out the fabric.

6 Peel the backing from the pinked circle and stick on top of the lid. Knot the ribbon around the lid in the same way as a school tie.

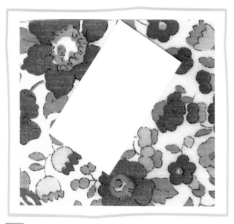

7 Select part of the fabric pattern suitable for a tag, and stick a larger piece of adhesive sheet behind it on the reverse of the fabric.

8 Turn the fabric to the front and cut out the chosen motif. Hold the motif onto a scrap of felt and cut around it to make felt backing for the fabric.

9 Remove the ribbon from the tin, and the paper backing from the fabric. Insert the ribbon's loose ends between the front and back of the tag, and press firmly together.

Cut a felt circle to fit inside the tin's base and stick in place with a small strip of self-adhesive tape.

Cut a thin piece of double-sided tape to stick inside the ribbon.

10 Stick the fabric rectangle to the main part of the tin. Re-attach the ribbon.

To customise a tin with felt fabric flowers, you will need:

Materials

- Double-sided adhesive sheet
- 100% cotton patterned pink fabric - 2 different designs
- 250ml (8oz) candle making tin with lid
- 60cm (24″) ribbon, 5mm (.2″) wide
- Deep pink and light pink felt fabric remnants
- 2 flower templates
- Optional: very small circle of self-adhesive foam sheet, using a hole punch
- Pair of compasses with pencil

Equipment

- Pinking shears
- Fabric scissors and craft scissors

1 Draw around the small template onto the reverse of one of the pink fabrics.

2 Draw round the large and small templates onto a piece of self-adhesive sheet. Cut out.

3 Cut out the patterned fabric flower.

Peel off the adhesive sheet's backing paper and stick the 2 flower shapes onto different coloured felt. Cut these out.

Cut small circles for the flower centres, backed with adhesive sheet. An alternative for the small flower is to press out a tiny circle of self-adhesive foam sheet for the centre, using a hole punch.

4 Cut out and stick the fabrics on and inside the tin as before (see above) and tie the ribbon in the same way. Sandwich the ribbon ends with the felt flower at the front of the tag, and the patterned flower behind. Stick the large felt flower on the lid.

Original Size

Materials

- Double-sided adhesive sheet
- 100% cotton patterned green fabric
- 250ml (8oz) candle making tin with lid
- Mushroom templates
- Red and white spotted fabric remnant
- Cream or yellow fabric remnant

Equipment

- Pair of compasses with pencil
- Pinking shears
- Fabric scissors and craft scissors

1 Draw around the whole mushroom templates onto a piece of adhesive sheet: 4 large mushrooms and 3 small ones.

2 Cut up the mushrooms to separate the cap and stem. Stick the stems onto the reverse of the cream or yellow fabric. Stick the caps on the spotted fabric.

3 Cut out the mushroom components.

4 Cut out and stick the fabrics on and inside the tin as before (see above). Peel the backing paper from the mushroom fabric pieces and stick on the background fabric.

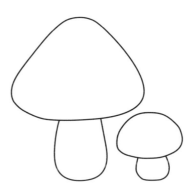

Original Size

Funny
Hoops

CONVIVIAL CATS

Create these friendly felines with just a little hand
sewing and some self - adhesive details.

TIP To join the foam pieces accurately, start by pressing together at the
top of the head, and gradually work downwards towards the legs; taking it
slowly produces better results.

Materials

- ☑ Heart, large shirt and large cat templates
- ☑ Circular template 23cm (9″) diameter
- ☑ 18cm (7″) embroidery hoop
- ☑ White self-adhesive foam sheet
- ☑ Remnants of felt fabric
- ☑ Lace or broderie anglaise trim
- ☑ 100% cotton fabric remnants in 2 designs
- ☑ Iron-on interfacing
- ☑ Stick-on googly eyes
- ☑ Sewing thread
- ☑ Embroidery floss / thread
- ☑ Iron-on fusible web 25mm (1″) wide
- ☑ Ribbon 5mm (.2″) wide
- ☑ All-purpose or fabric glue
- ☑ Small button
- ☑ Sheet of paper kitchen roll

Equipment

- ☑ Fabric scissors and craft scissors
- ☑ Pencil
- ☑ Black ball point pen
- ☑ Needle
- ☑ Iron for pressing
- ☑ Pins

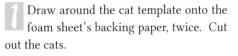

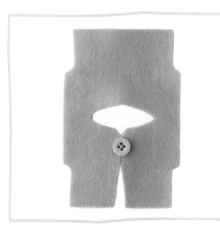

1 Draw around the cat template onto the foam sheet's backing paper, twice. Cut out the cats.

2 Remove the backing paper from both, and place one sticky surface on top of the other sticky surface exactly. There should now be a single cat comprising a double layer of foam.

Stick on the eyes and lightly draw the face and paws with a pencil.

3 Use the template to cut out the shirt from felt fabric, and sew the button in place.

4 Complete the facial features and paws with a ball point pen.

Put the felt shirt over the cat's head and pin it together at the sides. If your embroidery floss / thread contains 6 strands, separate them and insert 3 strands into the needle. Sew the sides of the shirt together in running stitch.

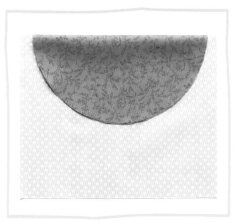

5 Use the circular template to cut out the hoop's background fabric. Fold the fabric in half and draw round this semi-circle onto the reverse of a second piece of fabric.

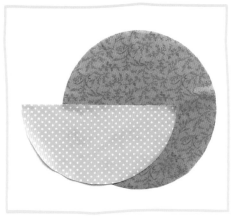

6 Cut out the semi-circle and open out the background fabric.

7 Fold over 5mm (.2″) of fabric on the right side of the semi-circle's straight edge, and press with an iron.

Fold a strip of fusible web lengthways and place it under the trim, lifting both of them onto the top edge of the semi-circle. Iron the trim in place until fixed to the fabric.

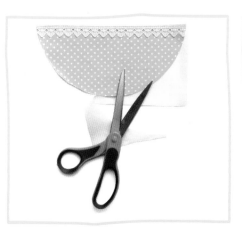

8 Iron interfacing onto the back of the semi-circle, and trim off the excess with scissors.

9 Cut out a heart from the felt fabric using the template. Place it centrally on the fabric pocket and put a small piece of fusible web underneath it. Lay a sheet of kitchen roll on top of the heart and press with an iron. The heart will then stay in place while you sew some running stitches with embroidery floss around the edge.

10 Place the semi-circular pocket on top of the background fabric. Cut a few short strips of fusible web lengthways and insert them between the pocket edge and the circle edge. Iron in place and allow to cool.

Fit the fabric into the embroidery hoop, and tighten the screw on the frame. Tie a ribbon to the frame and hang it up on a hook to see whether the pocket top is straight. If not, adjust the position of the fabric inside the hoop.

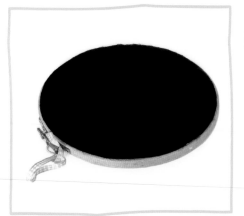

11 Sew running stiches along the raw edge of the fabric circle, pulling to gather the fabric as you go. Make several stitches on top of each other at the beginning and end so that the thread is fastened securely.

12 For the back, cut a circle of felt fabric slightly smaller than the outer hoop. Squeeze a line of glue where the gathered fabric meets the outer hoop, all the way round. Press the felt circle in place to finish. (Glue soaking through the felt is less noticeable on a dark colour.)

13 Slip the cat into its pocket.

14 To make a smaller cat for company, use the templates for a 15cm (6") hoop and cut a circular template 20cm (8") in diameter. Otherwise, the instructions are the same.

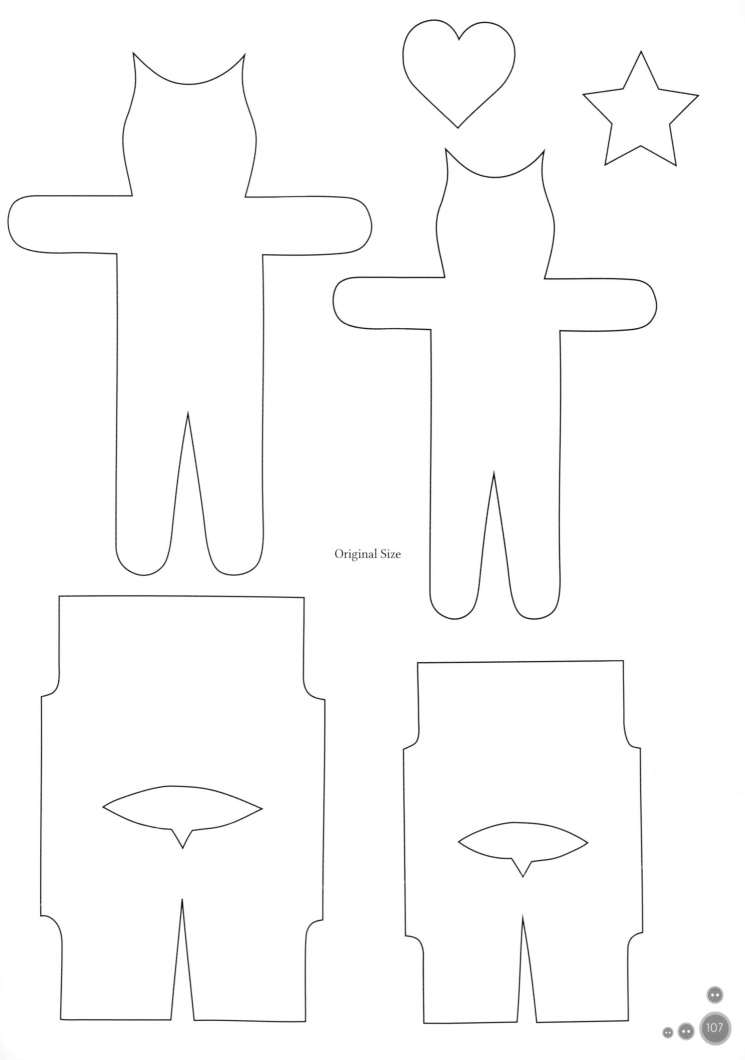

Original Size

HOOP EMBROIDERY

Transfer an outline onto fabric, and hand-sew
these cute pictures with basic stitches.

TIP To obtain a good quality image, photocopy the template first, and
attach the transfer sheet to it with paper clips before tracing.

To make a buzzing beehive embroidery, you will need:

Materials

- 100% white cotton fabric cut into a circle 18cm (7") diameter
- Iron-on interfacing cut into a circle 13cm (5") diameter
- Tracing paper or transfer paper
- Embroidery floss / thread in yellow, black, pale blue, mauve and orange
- White sewing thread
- Small sheet of white card
- Embroidery hoop 13cm (5")

Equipment

- Iron-on transfer pencil
- Iron for pressing
- Needle
- Pair of compasses
- Pencil
- Scissors
- All-purpose glue

1 Iron the interfacing circle onto the centre of the fabric circle until they are fused together

Flip the fabric over so that the interfacing is underneath.

2 Trace the picture outline with the transfer pencil.

3 To transfer the picture, turn the tracing paper over and iron the back of it onto the centre of the fabric.

Place the fabric, picture upwards, in the embroidery hoop.

5 If your embroidery floss / thread comprises 6 strands, separate them so that you are stitching with just 3 strands at a time.

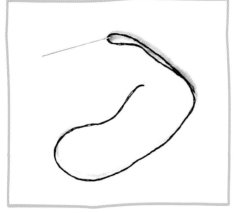

6 On the picture, the dot for the bees' eyes is stitched with a French knot.

After knotting the thread, push the needle from the back to the front of the fabric.

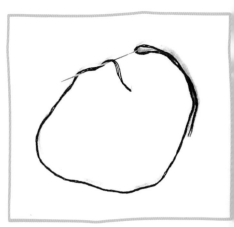

7 Wrap the thread twice around the needle.

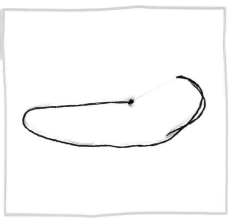

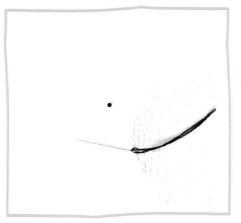

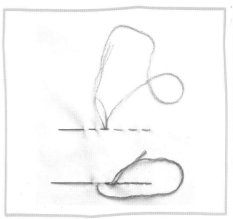

8 Push the needle back into the fabric at exactly the same place. As you do this, pull the thread taut and away from the needle.

9 With the thread still taut, push the needle through to the back of the fabric. You are then left with a French knot on the front.

10 On the embroidery picture, a broken line is sewn with running stitch. A running stitch goes in one direction, with gaps in between.

Solid lines on the picture are sewn in backstitch. The first stitch is a running stitch, but then the needle is taken backwards so that the thread can fill the gap. The needle goes forward again and then backwards to fill the next gap. This is repeated until the end of the line.

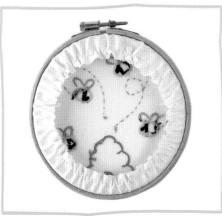

11 Complete the embroidery using French knots, running stitch and back stitch.

12 On the back, sew running stitches along the raw edge of the fabric circle, pulling to gather the fabric as you go.

13 Make several stitches on top of each other at the beginning and end, so that the thread is fastened securely.

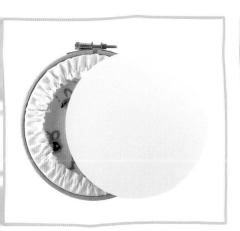

14 With compasses and a pencil, draw a circle onto card to fit the back of the hoop, and cut it out. Squeeze glue where the gathered fabric meets the outer hoop, all the way round. Stick the card in place.

15 You can also stitch a flower and dragonfly embroidery following the same instructions.

16 The colours used this time are blue, purple, red, orange, yellow and green.

PLAY CUSHION

A soft, huggable cushion that
can be thrown and caught.

TIP When you have finished drawing around the
template, cut just inside this outline so that it is not
seen on the finished item.

Materials

- 2 rectangles of felt fabric, 45cm x 65cm (18″ x 26″) each
- Jigsaw template
- Polyester filling or stuffing fibre

Equipment

- Fabric scissors
- Pins
- Sewing machine, threaded
- Pencil

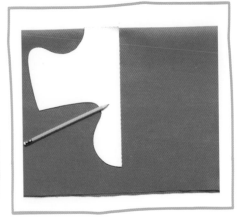

1 Fold one felt rectangle in half along its width. Place the template on the fabric with the shortest straight edge on the fold, and the longest straight edge in the middle of the fabric.

Draw around the curved edge of the template onto the fabric with a pencil.

2 Flip the template over and draw around the curved edge again.

3 There is now a half-jigsaw shape on the fabric. Pin the fabric in several places to keep it in position.

4 Cut along the pencil outline through 2 layers of fabric.

5 Unfold the fabric to see the whole jigsaw shape.

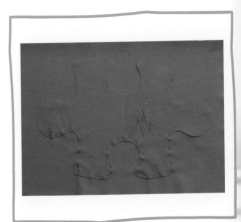

6 Pin the jigsaw shape on top of the second felt rectangle. Ensure that any pencil marks will not be seen from the front.

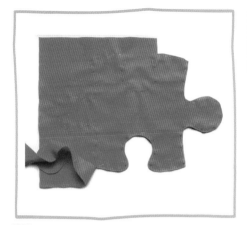

7 Use the jigsaw-shaped felt as a template for cutting the remaining fabric.

8 There are now 2 jigsaw shapes pinned together, ready to stitch. Adjust the pins so that they point away from the direction of sewing.

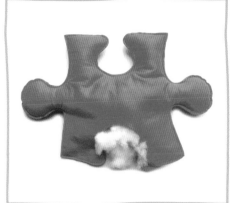

9 Machine stitch about 6mm (.25") away from the cushion edge, leaving a gap at the bottom for the stuffing.

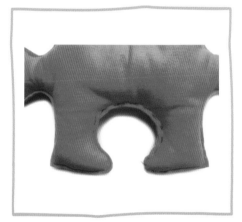

10 Stuff the cushion loosely, and pin the gap together.

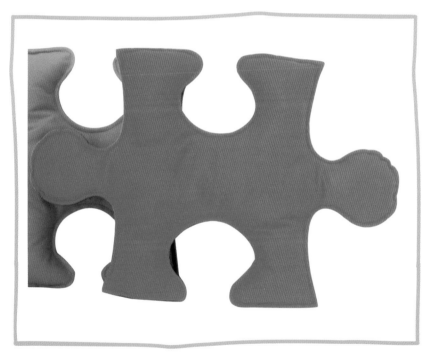

11 Sew the pinned section so that there is one continuous line of machine stitching all the way round the cushion.

RainBow Toy Bag and
FISHING GAME

The fabric fish on this attractive toy bag can be detached and hooked with rods in a game of skill and dexterity.

TIP When painting the rods, do one half at a time and stand in an empty mug while the top part dries.

To make the
bag and game,
you will need:

Materials

- Large drawstring bag 50cm x 75cm (20″ x 30″)
- Fish template
- 100% cotton fabric remnants in 7 rainbow colours
- 7 mini buttons in assorted colours
- Sewing threads
- Polyester stuffing or filling fibre
- Stick-on hook and loop tapes, about 1.2m (1.3 yds) of each type
- Ribbon in 7 colours to match the fabric, 5mm (.2″) wide, cut into 10cm (4″) lengths
- Emulsion paint in 2 bright colours
- 2 net curtain hooks
- 2 x 30cm (12″) wooden dowel rods, 12mm (.5″) thick

Equipment

- Pencil or ball point pen
- Fabric scissors
- Pins
- Sewing machine, threaded
- Needle
- Iron for pressing
- Bradawl
- Small decorators' paintbrush

1 Fold each remnant along the grain of the fabric, inside out, and insert a few pins to keep it in place. Draw around the template with a ball point pen or pencil on one side of the folded fabric. Cut out the two pieces with fabric scissors.

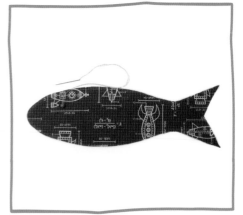

2 Hand-sew a button for the eye on one of the pieces.

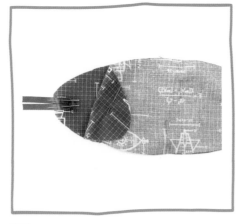

3 Place the right sides of the fish together so that the reverse of the fabric is on the outside. Pin back the front of the fish on one side. Fold over a length of ribbon to make a loop in the middle, and pin the loop on the fabric so that it's inside the fish. The ribbon ends should be 3cm (1.2″) outside the fabric edge.

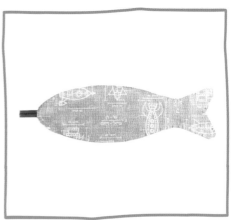

4 Pin the sides of the fish together all the way round.

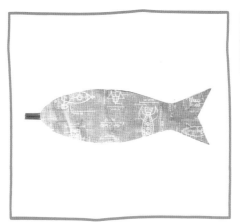

5 Machine stitch together, 5mm (.2″) away from the edge. Leave a gap at the bottom for the filling.

At the tail ends, trim the pointed tips to make them shorter and rounded.

Snip the fabric seam at intervals, almost up to the stitching line. Where the stitching bends or changes direction sharply, add more cuts.

6 Turn each fish outside in, carefully pushing the shape out with closed scissor blades. Press lightly with an iron.

Insert stuffing fibre into the fish via the gap in the seam, to gently plump it out. Slip-stitch the gap closed.

7 Cut a 15cm (6″) length of loop tape, peel off the liner, and stick it along the back of the fish. The top of the tape should be 2.3cm (1″) from the front end of the fish.

Complete all 7 fish in the same way.

8 Stick corresponding strips of hook tape about 15cm (6″) above the bottom of the cotton bag, positioning vertically.

9 Attach the fish to the bag in rainbow colour order.

10 Brush 2 coats of emulsion paint onto each dowel rod.

11 Pierce one end of the rod with a bradawl and twist a hook into the hole. Insert the bradawl in the hook and turn several times to tighten it.

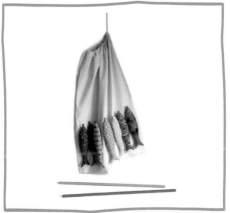

12 The fish can be detached from the bag to play a game hooking the loops with the fishing rods. When not in use, the rods can be stored in the bag with other toys.

Back to SCHOOL Projects

Brilliant school accessories to brighten up the new term.

TIP Instead of drawing a rabbit face on the pencil topper, you could just stick on two googly eyes.

Materials

☑ 3 waste cores from large adhesive tape rolls

☑ Adhesive tape

☑ Brown kraft wrapping paper

☑ Pencil templates

☑ Glue stick

☑ Recycled cardboard remnant, medium thickness that can be cut with scissors

☑ Double-sided clear adhesive tape, 15mm (.6″) wide

☑ Self-adhesive craft foam in assorted colours including white

Equipment

☑ Scissors

☑ Pencil

☑ Ruler

☑ Pair of compasses

1 Either tear off or stick down any loose bits of paper on the waste cores.

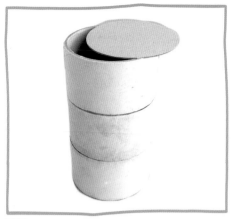

2 Stick three waste cores together by gluing the rims, forming one tube. Cut out two pieces of grey cardboard to fit one end of the tube, and glue them together to form a sturdy base.

3 Add tape to the joins in the tube. Glue the rim at one end and stick on the cardboard base.

Out of brown kraft paper, cut a piece to fit inside the tube, slightly short of the top, and so that the ends overlap inside. With compasses, draw a circle on brown paper slightly smaller than the base, and cut out. Put these two pieces to one side.

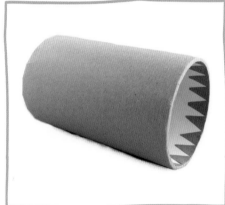

4 Cut a rectangle from the brown paper so that it is 4cm (1.6″) longer than the tube, and able to wrap around the outer circumference with an overlap. On the short ends of this rectangle, cut 'V' shapes out of the paper 2cm (.8″) deep.

Glue one long edge and both short edges of the brown paper. Fit around the tube, tucking the top inside and the bottom of the paper onto the base.

5 Stick the brown paper circle on the base to cover the 'V' shapes.

6 On the paper you previously cut for the inside of the tube, stick double-sided tape along the top and down one side on the outside. Insert into the tube to fit, and peel back the tape slowly at the top as you press the paper into place just under the rim. Near the end, unpeel the tape on the seam as well, and finish sticking the lining paper in position.

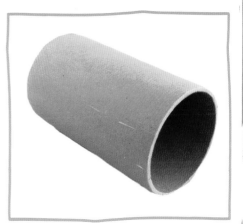

7 Your tube should now be completely covered in brown paper.

8 Draw the template for the whole pencil on the back of the coloured foam sheets to give you about 25 pencils in total. Cut out the whole pencils.

9 Then cut away the shaded area on the template. This will be where the white pieces go.

10 Draw around the whole template for the white inserts onto the back of the white foam sheet. With the pencil and ruler, draw a line on the foam sheet so that you can cut off the shaded area.

11 Cut off the white sections inside the pencil lines.

12 You should now have three different components for each pencil: the long part you hold, the 'wood' and the pencil point.

13 Remove the foam's backing paper and attach each of your three-part pencils to the outside of the tube, as shown, pressing firmly in place. Arrange so that they are evenly spaced.

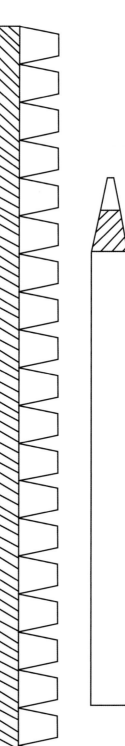

Original Size

To customise an A4 (8.5″ x 11″) notebook, you will need:

Materials

- Recycled cardboard remnant, medium thickness that can be cut with scissors
- Assorted washi tape rolls
- Double sided adhesive sheet
- Elephant template
- A4 (8.5″ x 11″) notebook

Equipment

- Craft scissors
- Pencil

1 Draw around the template both ways onto cardboard, and cut out two elephants.

2 Arrange the washi tape rolls in the order you want them to appear on the elephant.

3 Stick the first piece of tape vertically near the middle of the elephant.

4 Where the sides of the elephant are straight, fold the tape onto the back. Where the sides are curved, make small cuts in the tape on the reverse of the elephant.

5 Then press the tape down, ensuring that it follows the outline of the elephant closely.

6 Continue applying tape either side of the first strip, fitting the strips closely together.

Where the tape has to stick to a corner of the elephant's foot, cut a right-angled notch in it before folding to the back.

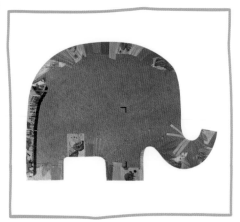  

7 The back of your elephant will look like this.

8 Add tape to the second elephant in the same way. Vary the order of some colours so that they look good when one animal is positioned above the other.

9 Draw around the template both ways onto one side of the adhesive sheet. Cut the shapes just inside the pencil line so that they are very slightly smaller than the washi taped elephants.

Remove the paper liner on one side and stick to the reverse of the taped elephants.

10 Before sticking, decide how you want to position the elephants on the book cover. Remove the remaining liner and stick down, pressing firmly.

Original Size

To make a rabbit pencil topper, you will need:

Materials

- Large wooden bead with hole about 9mm (.35") across
- A coloured pipe cleaner
- Narrow ribbon, 5-6mm (.2" - .25") wide
- Tube of clear all-purpose glue
- Pencil

Equipment

- Fine nibbed permanent marker
- Fabric scissors

1 Make 2 bends in the end of the pipe cleaner, as shown.

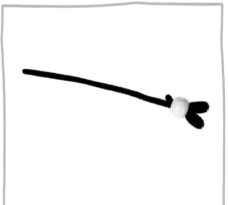

2 Insert the tops of the bends through the bead, leaving behind a short tail as well as the remaining length of pipe cleaner.

3 Twist the tail around the pipe cleaner length. Move the pipe cleaner to one side so that a pencil end can be inserted in the bead hole.

Squeeze glue into the bead hole.

4 Push the pencil into the hole and allow the glue to dry.

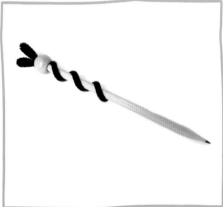

5 Twist the pipe cleaner firmly around the pencil.

6 With the fine nibbed marker, draw a simple rabbit face on the bead.

Knot the ribbon under the bead the same way as a school tie. Cut the ribbon ends into points with fabric scissors.

7 By choosing the bead, pencil and book cover in natural colours, the 2 finished items make an attractive matching set.

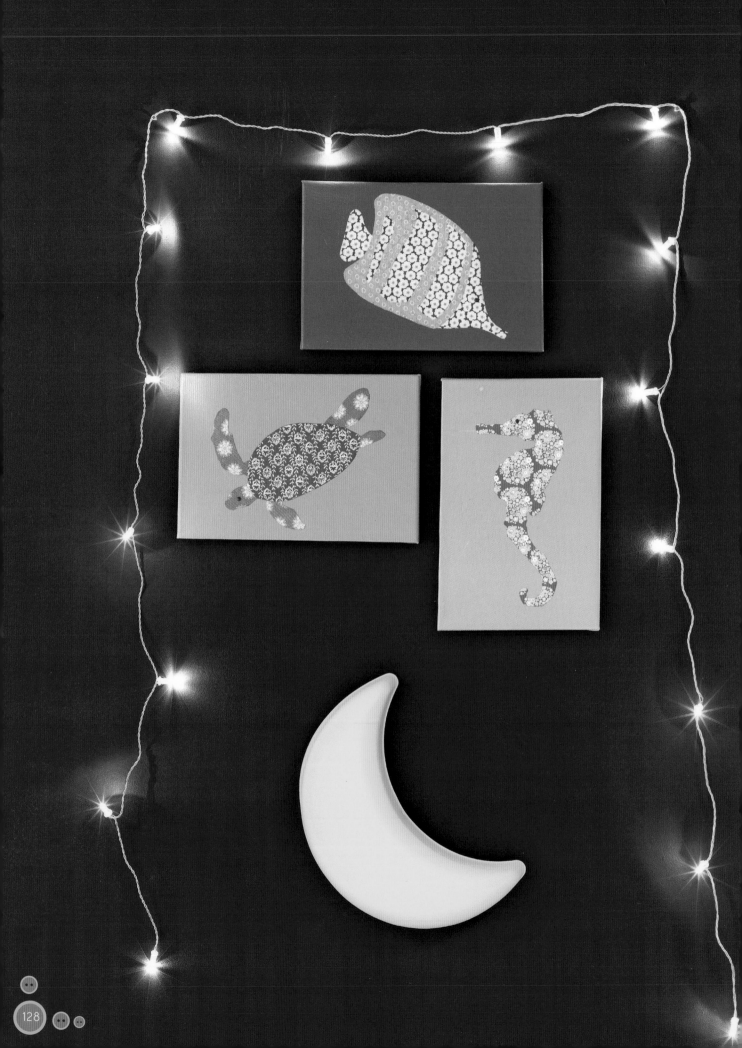

DEEP SEA

canvases

A pre-made canvas becomes art with a single
tube of acrylic paint, fabric and glue.

TIP When you have cut out the fabric shape, place it on the canvas before
you stick it down, to check that no unpainted areas are going to show.

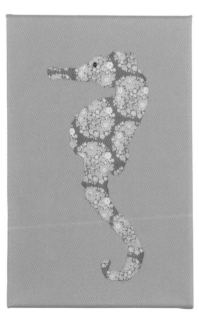

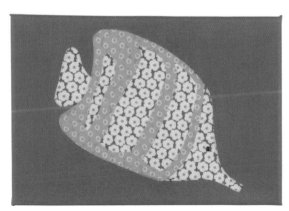

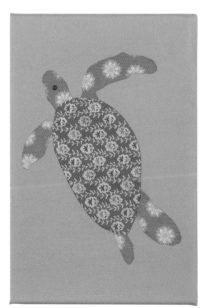

To make each picture, you will need:

Materials

- Primed blank canvas, 20cm x 30cm (8" x 12")
- Template
- Stick-on plastic gemstone
- Thick acrylic paint
- 100% cotton patterned fabric
- Decoupage glue, matt

Equipment

- Small decorators' paintbrush
- Pencil
- Fabric scissors and craft scissors

1 Draw around the template onto the centre of the canvas.

2 Brush a coat of paint onto the top and sides of the canvas, going slightly inside the drawn pencil lines.

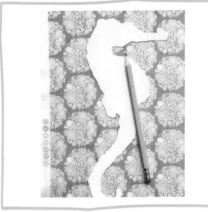

3 Draw around the template in reverse, onto the wrong side of the fabric.

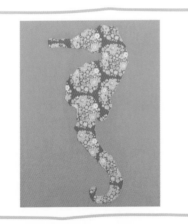

4 Cut out the fabric. Apply decoupage glue to the centre of the canvas and stick down the fabric shape. Allow to dry.

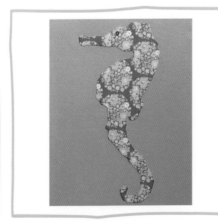

5 Paint a layer of glue on top of the fabric and the whole painted area except for the sides of the canvas. When dry, add a stick-on gemstone for the eye.

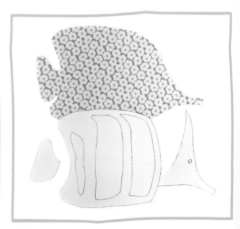

6 Where there are 2 different fabrics in the picture, use the whole template to cut out the background fabric. Then cut up the template ready for the top layer of fabric.

7 Stick the fish shape onto the painted canvas, as before.

8 Use the cut-up template to draw on the back of the second fabric. Remember to reverse the template first. Cut out the fabric.

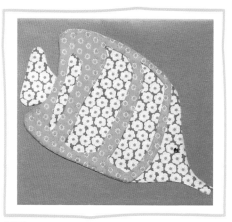

9 Stick down the second fabric. When dry, varnish the whole picture with glue and add the eye.

10 Again, use the whole template to cut out the turtle shape. Cut up the template afterwards so that just the shell part can be used.

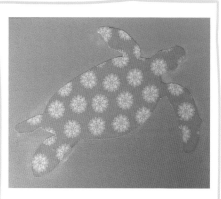

11 Stick the turtle on the painted canvas.

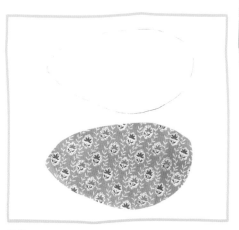

12 Use the shell template to cut out the second fabric.

13 Stick on the shell, and complete the picture as last time.

Rocking
HORSE
Picture

Use a pastry cutter to make and bake an
appealing picture from polymer clay.

TIP The clay comes away from the cutter more easily if you dip it in water
first, and if you don't roll out the clay too thickly.

Materials

White soft oven-bake polymer clay, around 350g (12.5oz) to enable 1 or 2 practice versions

Non-stick baking parchment

Acrylic paint

20cm x 20cm (8″ x 8″) white deep picture frame

100% cotton fabric remnants in two designs

Fusible web with paper backing

Card template 15cm x 15cm (6″ x 6″) square

Heavyweight iron-on interfacing

White mini-brad

Glue dots

Double-sided clear adhesive tape

Equipment

Rocking horse cookie cutter, large size

Adjustable rolling pin

Optional: polymer clay press

Pointed knife or clay tool

Knitting needle

Metal baking tray

Optional: oven thermometer

Metal nail file or fine glass-paper

Pencil

Fine artists' paintbrush (sable hair if possible)

Fabric scissors and craft scissors

Iron for pressing

Bradawl

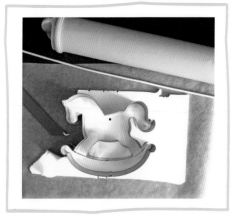

1 Roll out the polymer clay to a depth of about 2mm (.1″) using an adjustable rolling pin and baking parchment underneath.

Press the cookie cutter into the clay. Before removing the cutter, ensure that any excess clay at the edges is trimmed off with the knife or clay tool. Pierce a hole in the horse's back with the knitting needle.

2 Alternatively use a polymer clay press at a thick setting, then lift the clay onto the parchment. If the press leaves slight ridges in your clay, smooth over the surface once or twice with the rolling pin.

3 Trim the parchment closer to the clay shape, and transfer to the baking tray. Follow the manufacturer's instructions to bake or 'cure' the clay.

4 It is important to bake at the correct oven temperature. An inexpensive oven thermometer can be used if your heat controls are not completely accurate.

If the newly baked rocking horse curls a little as it cools, place a sheet of clean white paper on it, topped with a medium-sized book for an hour or so, to flatten it.

5 Smooth down any irregularities at the edges with the nail file.

Draw on the decorative design lightly with a pencil.

6 Complete in acrylic paint, as shown.

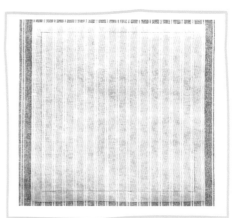

7 Draw around the square template onto the fusible web paper's smooth side. Cut about 1cm (.4″) outside the pencil lines. Place the web paper, smooth side up, onto the reverse of a fabric remnant. Line up the sides of the square with the grain of the fabric. Press with an iron so that the web is fused to the fabric.

8 Cut along the square's pencil outline. Remove the web's backing paper and put the fabric to one side.

9 Remove the back of the picture frame, and draw around this backing board onto the dull side of the heavyweight interfacing.

10 Cut out.

11 Place the interfacing's shiny side onto the reverse of the second fabric remnant. Line up the sides of the square with the grain of the fabric. Press with an iron to fuse the two together.

Trim the fabric close to the edge of the interfacing.

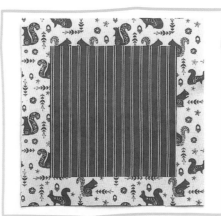

12 Place this larger fabric square right side up, and position the smaller fabric square centrally onto it, also right side up. Press together with the iron.

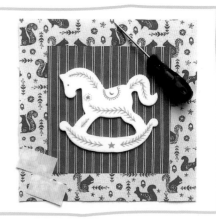

13 Stick a few glue dots at the back of the horse's curved rocker base to prevent it shifting out of place against the fabric background.

Position the rocking horse centrally onto the fabric background, and push the bradawl through its hole and through the fabric behind. Insert the mini-brad's two pins through this hole and open them up at the back of the fabric.

14 Apply double-sided tape to the inside of the picture's backing board, and remove the protective paper.

15 Press the fabric and rocking horse firmly onto the board.

Insert the board into the picture frame and fasten in place.

16 Turquoise and green comprise another colour combination suitable for any child's room.

BUTTONS and PATCHWORK Picture

A seam-free picture from offcuts, with a different
button hand-stitched onto every square.

TIP This project works best if you keep to a limited
colour scheme with the fabrics and buttons.

To make this picture, you will need:

Materials

- ✂ 15cm x 15cm (6″ x 6″) deep picture frame
- ✂ Light green emulsion paint
- ✂ Flower and large square templates
- ✂ Heavyweight iron-on interfacing
- ✂ 100% cotton fabric remnants: 9 different designs
- ✂ Sheet of kitchen paper roll
- ✂ 9 assorted buttons
- ✂ Double-sided adhesive tape

Equipment

- ✂ Small decorators' paintbrush
- ✂ Pencil
- ✂ Fabric scissors and craft scissors
- ✂ Iron for pressing
- ✂ Needle and thread

1 Dismantle the frame carefully, and put the glass somewhere safe. Paint only the parts you'll be able to see from the front when the frame is reassembled.

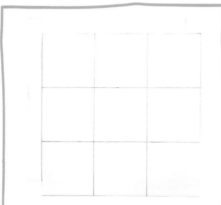

2 With a pencil, draw around the large square template onto the interfacing's dull side. Cut out with fabric scissors.

3 Cut out one of the small squares from the template.

4 Draw around this smaller template on the reverse of each of the patterned fabrics. Cut out the fabric on the inside of the pencil line to give you 9 different squares.

5 Decide how you want to arrange the 9 squares on the interfacing background. Leave the 4 corner pieces in place and put the others to one side.

Ensure that the corner squares line up exactly with the corners of the interfacing's shiny side. With an iron, press the fabric squares right side up onto the interfacing. Important - the hot iron must not touch the shiny surface of the interfacing.

6 Position the 4 squares that go between the corner pieces. Iron in place, avoiding the interfacing.

7 Add the final square, and iron the whole surface so that all of the fabric squares are stuck securely to the backing.

8 On a fresh piece of interfacing, dull side up, draw around the flower template 9 times leaving gaps in between the motifs.

9 You will still be able to see the flower shapes when you turn the interfacing over. On the shiny side, place small fabric pieces over the flower outlines.

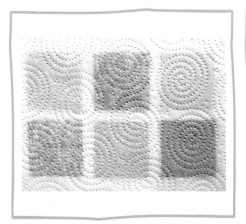

10 Place a sheet of kitchen roll onto the fabric pieces and shiny interfacing surface. Press the kitchen paper with the iron. Then turn over and iron the interfacing's dull side until the fabric is fused to it. (Don't worry about the paper being stuck as well.)

11 Allow the fabric to cool. Cut out the flowers.

12 Place one flower centrally onto a fabric square, and select a button. Sew on the button by pushing the needle through the flower, square, and backing. Repeat for each square.

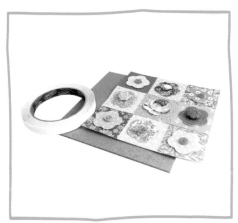

13 Fix the reverse of the interfacing onto the frame's backing board with double-sided tape. Reassemble the frame to complete the picture.

Stitch – Free
WALL HANGINGS

Make splendid fabric pictures without sewing a single stitch, using fusible web and decorative fasteners.

TIP For either picture, use the brightest coloured fabrics you can find so that they stand out against the background.

Materials

- Graph paper or plain paper rectangle measuring 27cm x 40cm (10.5″ x 15.75″)
- 50cm (20″) cotton herringbone tape, 25mm (1″) wide
- Navy blue felt fabric
- Craft brads: 3 white and 6 small black for the tabs
- Craft brads: 15 in white, yellow and red for the stars
- Rocket template
- Optional: 2 star templates, if you don't use craft punches
- Assorted patterned fabrics including yellows, dark blue, orange or red, spots and stripes
- White card thin enough to go through a photocopier or printer
- Glue stick
- Double-sided clear adhesive tape
- 30cm (12″) wooden dowel rod, 12mm (.5″) diameter
- Blue emulsion paint

Equipment

- Ruler
- White dressmakers' pencil
- Pinking shears
- Scissors
- Bradawl
- Colour photocopier
- Pencil
- Optional: large and small star punches, or use templates and cut them out by hand
- Small decorators' paintbrush

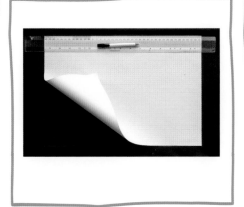

1 Place the paper rectangle on the felt fabric. Use a ruler to help draw round the paper with a white dressmakers' pencil.

2 Cut the fabric with pinking shears outside the white line. Turn the fabric right way up so that the line is on the reverse.

3 Cut 3 tabs from the herringbone tape, each 14cm (5.5″) long, and fold in half.

4 Place the folded tapes behind the fabric panel. Pierce the fabric and tape with a bradawl, and secure the tape in place with 3 brads. The middle brad should be white.

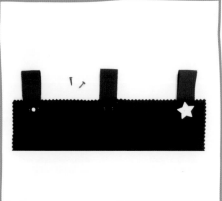

5 On white card, either stamp out 3 small stars with a craft punch, or draw around the small star template 3 times and cut them out by hand. Pierce the centre of the stars with a bradawl.

Remove the white brads, insert them through the stars, and replace them under the tabs.

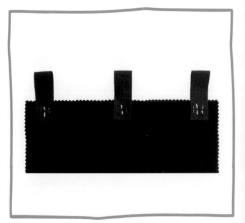

6 This is what the opened-out brads should look like from the back.

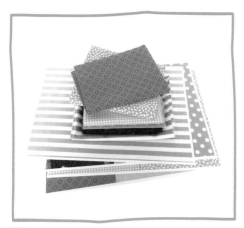

7 Place patterned fabric on the glass plate of a photocopier, one or two at a time. Make colour photocopies of the fabric onto white card.

8 Draw round the rocket template on the striped paper, and cut out.

9 Cut up the template so that you are left with the round window, nose-cone and fins.

Draw round the window onto the dark blue paper, and the other pieces on the spotted paper.

10 Cut out these smaller shapes and stick them onto the rocket.

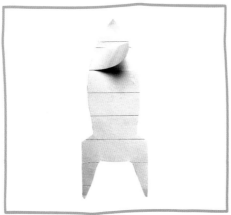

11 Stick double-sided tape onto the back of the rocket.

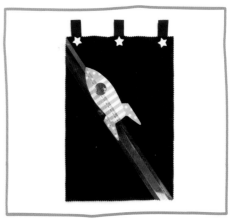

12 Use a ruler to position the rocket on the diagonal.

13 Peel off the tape's backing paper and stick the rocket to the felt background.

14 For the stars under the rocket, either use a craft punch or draw round the templates.

15 Pierce the card stars with a bradawl, and press the brads through the holes.

16 Push the bradawl through the fabric where the first star will be placed.

17 Insert a star and brad into the fabric, and open the brad at the back. Continue until there are about 15 large and small stars under the rocket.

18 Paint two coats of emulsion onto the wooden rod.

19 Push the painted rod through the tabs. Tap 2 small nails into a wall and hang the rod onto them.

To make an exotic flower panel, you will need:

Materials

- 100% cotton patterned fabric for the background 27cm x 40cm (10.6″ x 15.75″)
- Heavyweight iron-on interfacing 27cm x 40cm (10.6″ x 15.75″)
- 100% cotton fabric remnants for the tablecloth, plant pot, leaves and stems (3 or 4 different greens), and flower head (pink and red)
- Templates for the tablecloth, plant and pot
- Fusible web with paper backing
- Iron-on fusible web strip, 25mm (1″) wide
- 50cm (20″) cotton herringbone tape, 25mm (1″) wide
- 30cm (12″) wooden dowel pole, 15mm (.5″) diameter
- Emulsion paint
- 3 craft brads

Equipment

- Iron for pressing
- Fabric scissors and craft scissors
- Pencil
- Small decorators' paintbrush
- A pin
- Bradawl

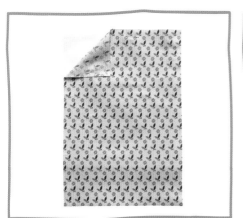

1 Iron the fabric onto most of the interfacing until they are fused together. Leave the top open for now.

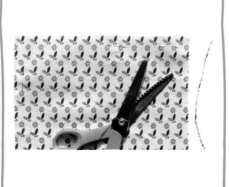

2 With pinking shears, cut the fabric edge.

3 Cut 3 tabs from the herringbone tape, each 14cm (5.5″) long, and fold in half.

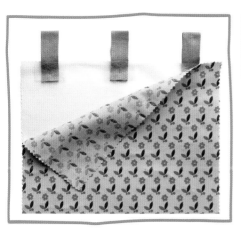

4 Place the folded tape on the interfacing, and lay some fusible web across the bottom of the tape.

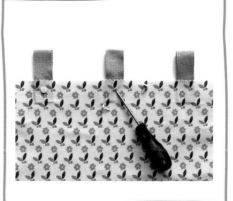

5 Replace the fabric on the interfacing and iron together so that the tape is fixed in place. Pierce through the fabric and tape with a bradawl, and insert a brad under each tab.

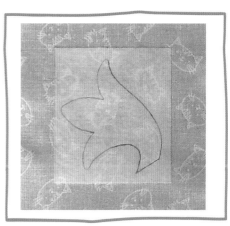

6 Draw around the plant and pot templates onto the smooth side of the fusible web paper, leaving spaces in between. Cut around the shapes, not on the pencil outlines.

7 With the smooth sides of the paper upwards, iron the shapes onto the reverse of the cotton fabric remnants.

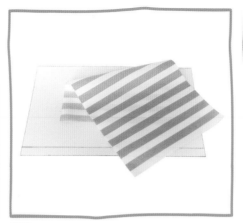

8 Use the whole template to cut the tablecloth fabric. Then cut the strip off the template and draw around it onto the fusible web paper.

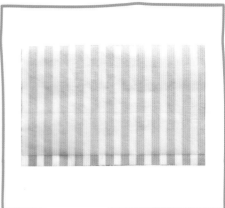

9 Iron the web paper onto the reverse of the tablecloth.

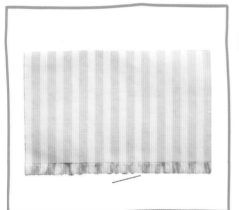

10 With a pin, pull some threads from the bottom of the tablecloth to make a fringe.

11 You should now have these fabric pieces cut from the templates. Remove the backing papers.

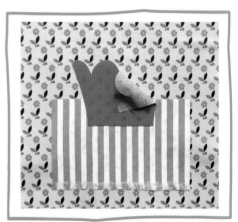

12 On the panel front, place the tablecloth about 3cms (1.2″) above the bottom edge, positioning centrally. Press with an iron to fuse it to the panel. Add the plant pot, but iron only the base of it for now.

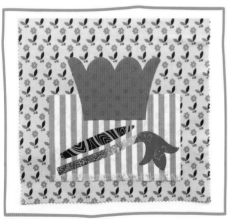

13 Arrange a right-facing flower and a small leaf on the tablecloth, as shown. Once the flower head is in the correct position, move the stem pieces aside and iron on the flower. Iron on the stem parts one by one, ensuring they fit closely together, and then the separate leaf.

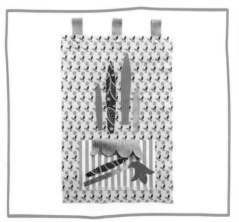

14 Arrange the remaining leaves and flowers. When satisfied with their positions, remove the flowers and iron the leaves in place.

15 This time, complete the flowers by starting with the dark green stem base, ensuring that it is vertical. (For the shorter flower, you may need to snip off some of the stem base.) Then piece by piece, iron the rest of the flower down. Finally, iron the top of the plant pot in place, over the stem and leaf bases.

Allow the panel to cool in a flat position.

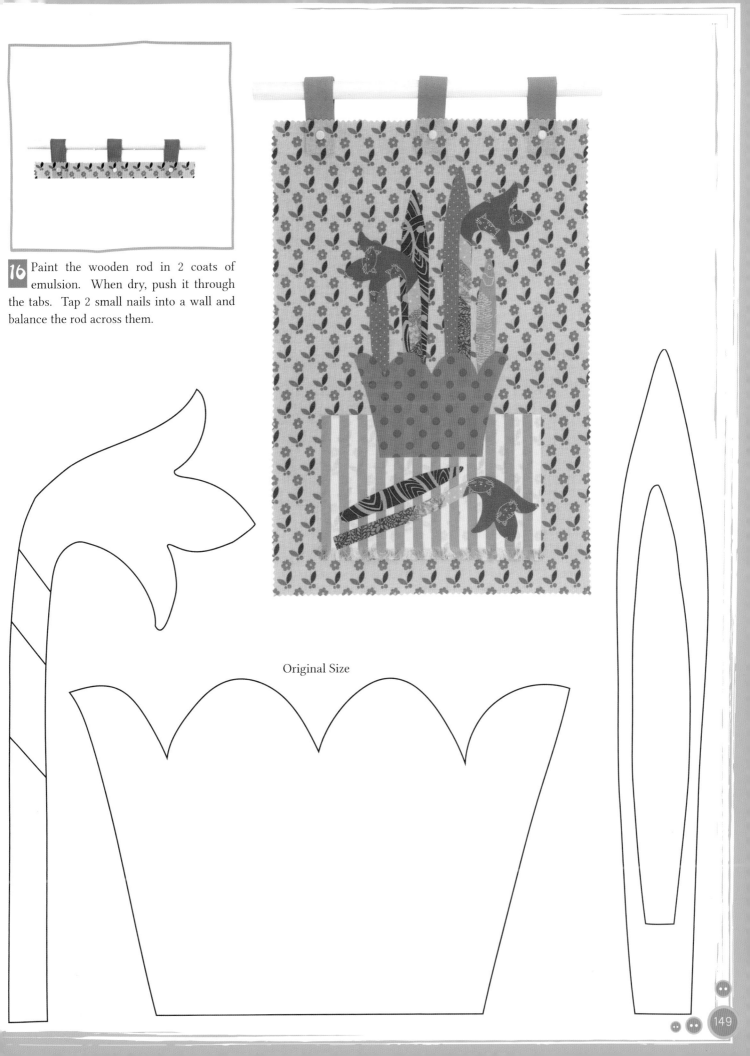

16 Paint the wooden rod in 2 coats of emulsion. When dry, push it through the tabs. Tap 2 small nails into a wall and balance the rod across them.

Original Size

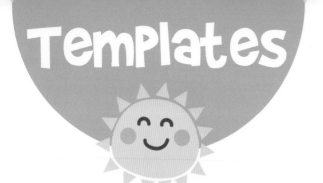

Templates

For some projects you need to make a template at the beginning. It's a quick and easy way to get a good result.

How to make a template using a photocopier (or scanner)

1 Find the template in this book that relates to your project
2 Place the page face-down on the copier's glass plate and close the lid
3 Print the template in black and white onto a piece of card thin enough to go through the machine
4 Cut along the template's outline with good quality craft scissors
5 The card template is now ready to use in your project

How to make a template without a photocopier

1 Find the template in this book that relates to your project
2 Place some tracing paper over the template
3 Trace the template with a sharpened pencil
4 Turn the tracing paper over and shade where you can see pencil lines
5 Turn the paper right way up again, and attach it to a piece of card with a clip
6 Go over the traced lines with a sharpened pencil or a ball point pen, pressing quite hard
7 Remove the paper and you will see an outline
8 Cut out the shape and your template is ready to use

How to make a rectangular template

1 With a pencil and ruler, draw the size of rectangle you want onto a sheet of graph paper, using the printed guidelines to help you
2 Photocopy the rectangle onto a piece of card
3 Cut out the card template
4 If you have no copier, glue the paper onto the card and cut them out together

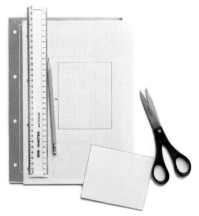

How to make a circular template

1 You will need a pair of compasses and a pencil, a piece of card that is easy to cut with scissors, and a ruler
2 Open the compasses to measure half the diameter of the template you need
3 Draw a circle on the card
4 Cut out the circle with scissors

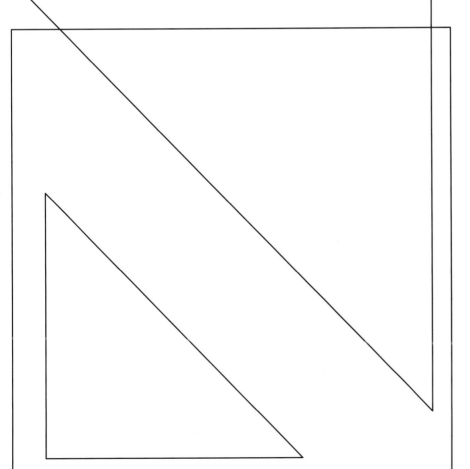

Seam – Free

Patchwork Cushions

Page 24

Original Size

Pocket Prehistorics and Pets

Page 30

Original Size

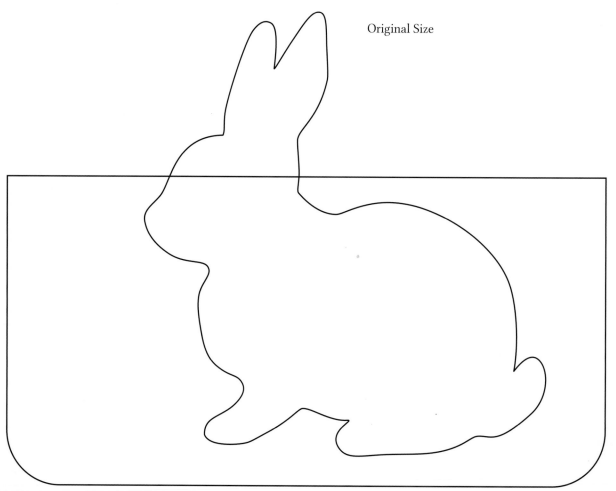

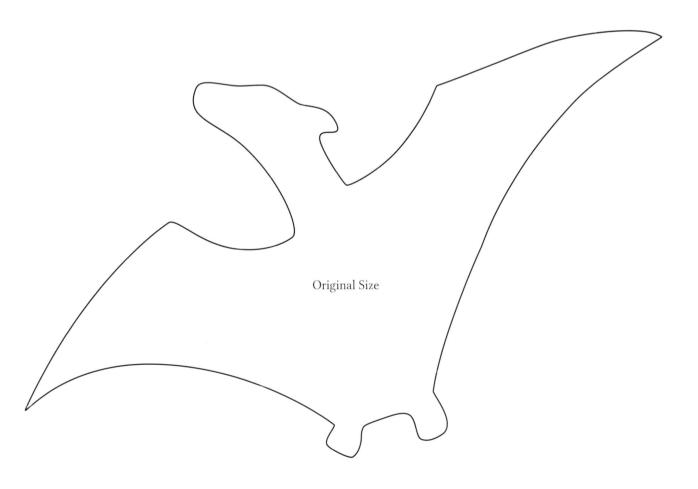

Original Size

Play Cushion

Page 112

Original Size

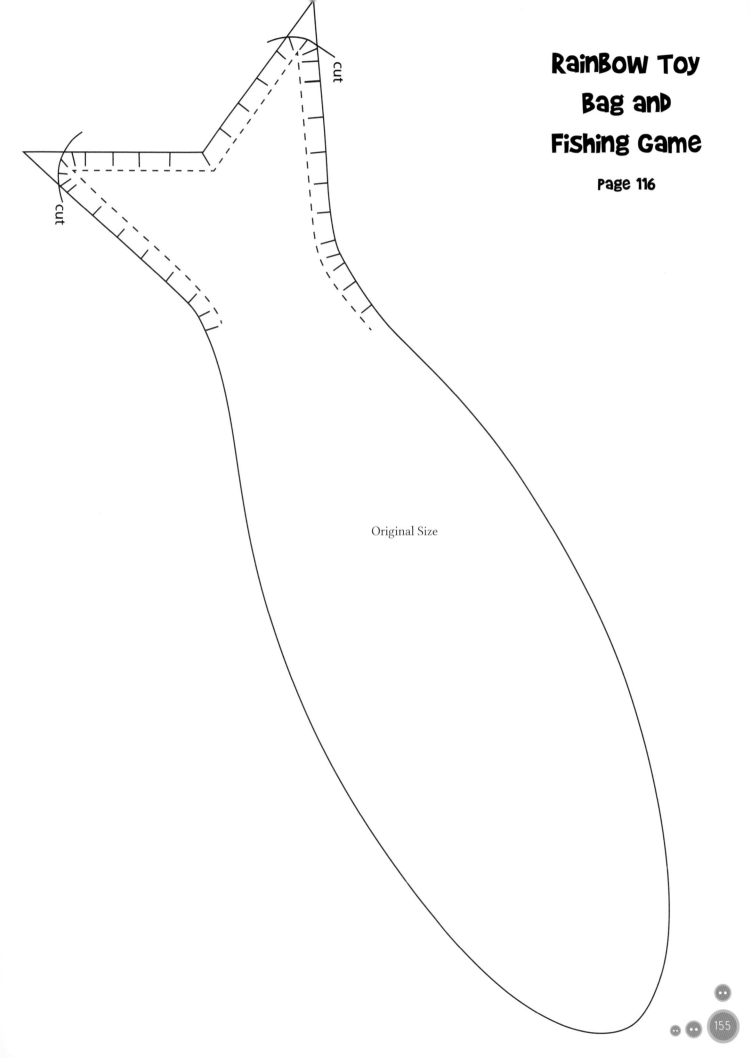

RainBow Toy
Bag and
Fishing Game

Page 116

cut

cut

Original Size

155

Deep
Sea Canvases
Page 128

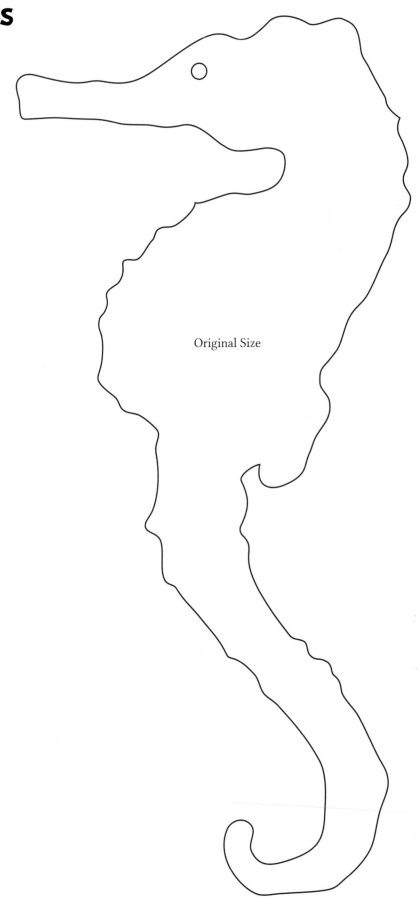

Original Size

Original Size

Deep
Sea Canvases

Page 128

Original Size

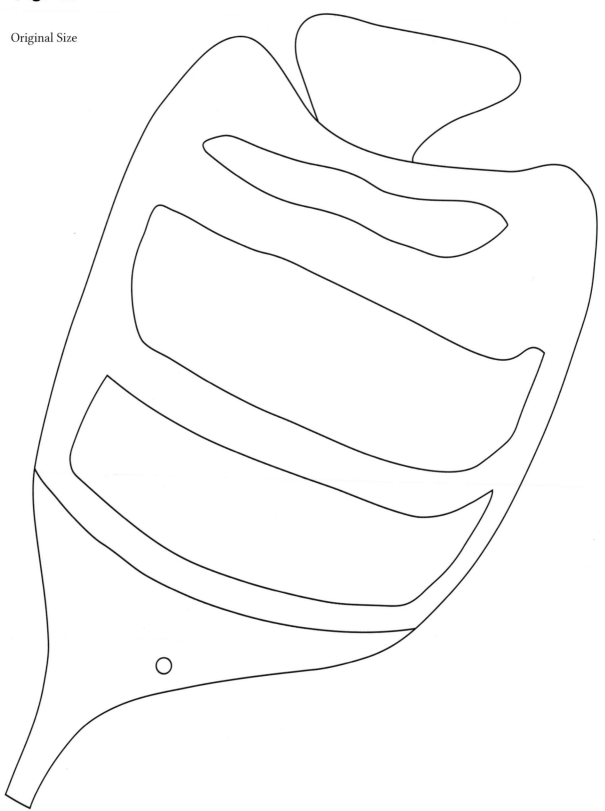

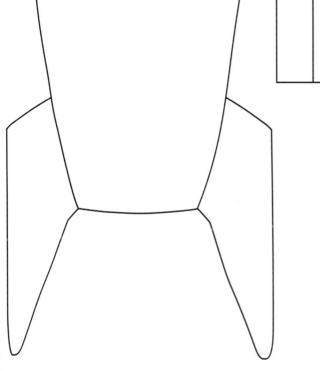

Stitch – Free
Wall
Hangings

Page 142

Original Size

Buttons and Patchwork Picture

Page 139

Original Size

HOOP Embroidery

Page 108

Original Size